BLIND TRUST

BLIND TRUST

...eed and murder shattered the serenity of an affluent Ohio village and set police on a frantic quest to find the killers

A TRUE CRIME STORY

FRANK P. STILES

Outskirts Press, Inc.
Denver, Colorado

In memory of Velma Bush and Harriett Wernert

To the men and women in blue who guard our streets, homes, and lives while we take for granted the blessings we enjoy. It is they who put themselves in harm's way to protect our rights and well-being.

Bravo to our legal system, the judges, prosecutors, and defense attorneys who not only protect the rights of the abused but those of the accused. Although no system is perfect, ours is the best in the world.

Acknowledgements

In the writing of this book, I owe many thanks to:

- The officers of the Ottawa Hills police department who assisted with the investigation that led to the arrest of those responsible for the brutal murders of Velma Bush and Harriett Wernert.
- All the Lucas County prosecutors: Anthony G. Pizza, Darrell Van Horn, Henry G. Harris, David O. Bauer, James D. Bates, and Robert J. Gilmer, who so diligently brought justice to the victims and their families.
- Special thanks to Ottawa Hills' retired Chief of Police Edward Lloyd Wechtel, who not only directed the officers in his department during this trying time, but also was my investigative partner in this case.
- Cover art: Jake Jones - Illustration and Design, Sylvania, Ohio
- Toledo police department scientific investigation unit

director, Keefe Snyder, for taking some of the photographs in the book.

- Retired Toledo Blade newspaper editor Tom Gearhart, and journalist Jim Eckstrom, managing editor of The Times Herald newspaper in Olean, New York, for their assistance during the writing of this book.
- John Robinson Block and the Toledo Blade newspaper for research information obtained from their newspaper morgue.
- The Toledo-Lucas County Public Library System and the library's Local History and Genealogy Department staff for their assistance in finding some of the information used in this book.
- The Lucas County Clerk of Courts - and Coroner's Office - for providing public records.
- Chief Robert Overmeyer and Sergeant Scott Steinke of the Ottawa Hills Police Department for providing some past police records pertaining to the murder investigation.
- And of course my beautiful wife B.J Stiles, who encourages my writing and makes my life fulfilling.

Prologue

The murders of 67-year-old Harriett Wernert and her 97-year-old mother, Velma Bush, in the confines of their own home shocked the quiet, affluent village of Ottawa Hills. It also demonstrated that evil can occur in any community. There had never been a murder in this small village, located on the edge of Toledo in northwest Ohio.

The murders sent shock waves through the village as residents pressed local police for answers and scurried to find ways to protect themselves. Additional deadbolts and security systems were added, and some residents purchased guns.

The village Chief of Police looked to the city of Toledo's Police Department for help, and because of my investigative experience I was assigned to assist in the search for answers.

The ensuing investigation, arrests, and trials of the three murderers, held simultaneously in three Common Pleas courtrooms, is packed with suspense.

1

Where It All Began

Harriett Wernert and her mother, Velma Bush, resided at 2130 Emkay Drive in the village of Ottawa Hills, Ohio, a scenic and quiet setting, known to be a safe community. After all, there was hardly any crime in the village and never murder.

The village, with a population of 4,500, took its name from the Ottawa Indians who settled in the area during the early 1700s. Known for its beautiful landscaping, flower gardens, suburban Colonial and French architectural homes, wealthy families migrated to the village to escape the bustle of big-city life.

This suburb of Toledo, Ohio, was founded and developed in 1915 by John North Willys, owner and president of Willys-Overland Motor Company, the second largest producer of automobiles in the United States between 1912 and 1918.

The two square-mile village offers residents a nearby golf course, beautiful parks, and a public school district that still is the second best in Ohio. Although the crime rate was exceptionally low the village does maintain its own police department consisting of the

Chief of Police, ten full-time and four part-time officers. They also have their own fire department and rescue squad and are, for the most part, a self-sufficient community.

The village itself isn't cluttered with restaurants and malls, but there are fine dining and excellent shops nearby. Many major highways are accessible and the University of Toledo is nestled on the outskirts.

The village government consists of a part-time mayor and six part-time councilmen. At the time Velma Bush and Harriett Wernert lived in the village, the municipal court judge was Richard Secor, and the village prosecutor was Robert Dorrell. They presided over misdemeanor cases and preliminary hearings concerning felony cases.

Harriett and Velma lived in their home with Harriett's husband James, who purchased the house in 1954. Harriett and James had a biological son, David Ernest Wernert, and an adopted son, James Scott Wernert.

David graduated from the University of Toledo's School of Business Administration. He had been a member of ROTC and after graduation he joined U.S. Army ordnance unit as a second lieutenant.

He married his wife Patricia at St. Andrew's Church in Toledo on June 17, 1961, a few days after she graduated from Monroe (Mich.) High School. Patricia gave birth to their only child, David James Wernert, on Sept. 16, 1963, and they were a military family until August 1969, when David was honorably discharged. They took up residence at 2009 Christie St. in Toledo, a home owned by his grandmother, Velma Bush.

Harriett's adopted son, James, and his wife Deborah, moved to San Bernardino, California.

Harriett's husband died in 1972, leaving the widow and her mother living alone in the Emkay Drive home. In 1974 her son David went to work at Will Dennis Volkswagen, a dealership in Toledo; as an auto parts manager.

Patricia Wernert was employed as a receptionist at Trilby Animal Hospital. She and David were also good friends with her boss, Dr. Robert Burns, and his wife Donna.

In 1975, Harriett Wernert was 67 and Velma Bush was 97.

James Wernert Sr. was a manufacturer's representative and president of the former Car Parts Warehouse, while Harriett volunteered in the gift shop at Toledo Hospital.

Before he died in 1951, Velma Bush's husband, Henry Bush, was secretary-treasurer of Oberly Enameling Company. Velma didn't work and in 1975, at age 97, she was getting frail and used a walker. Harriett's health was also deteriorating, but she still drove and maintained their home. The ladies attended St. Andrew's Episcopal Church and remained living alone with Harriett's black French poodle, "Frenchie." The ladies had a net worth of around $700,000, and they owned their two homes. At Velma's death most everything would go to Harriett, and at the time of her death, the remaining inheritance would go to her sons, David and James.

David would come over occasionally to check on his mother and grandmother and tend to their needs. Even though their health was failing, they enjoyed life in this serene neighborhood. Their neighbors, friends, and fellow churchgoers spoke well of Harriett and Velma. The village was a great place to grow old – or so they thought.

2

Silencing Of The Innocent

When Harriett Wernert crawled out of bed around 7 a.m. on Tuesday, Nov. 18, 1975, the house on Emkay Drive was chilly. The mercury dropped during the night to 28 degrees and the sparkling crystals of frost on the windows were a sure sign that winter was not far away.

Still in her bedclothes, pink slippers and a blue robe, Harriett made her way toward the kitchen to start the coffee. Her mother Velma Bush would stay in bed until Harriett called for her to come to breakfast and take her morning medicine.

Mom, "Its time to get up," Harriett called. It wasn't long before she heard the familiar shuffling of Velma's feet coming from her bedroom through the dining room to the kitchen. Sometimes Velma used a walker but lately she was without it much of the time. Wearing a wig, brown straight pullover dress, half nylon stockings, and low wide-heel shoes, Velma was dressed for the day.

Even though the house had an upstairs and a basement, the ladies never used them; they lived on the first floor. The ground level had three bedrooms, a dining room, living room, kitchen, laundry room connected to the kitchen, and two and a half bathrooms. A door from the laundry room accessed the two car garage where Harriett kept her red 1970 Ford Mustang.

Her son David also stored his Triumph racing car in her garage. David and his wife Patricia both had Triumph racing cars, but Patricia kept hers at their house. They belonged to Team Baron Racing Club, which was affiliated with Fiasco, a national racing organization.

David also used his mother's basement to store car parts and tires. He was really the only person to go into the basement unless a repairman needed to get to the furnace or hot water heater.

Velma's bedroom, the dining room, and the kitchen are in a direct line with one another, connected by archways and doorways. Harriett's bedroom and the spare bedroom are located across from each other and just beyond Velma's bedroom. All three of the bedrooms are accessible to each other by a connecting hallway.

"Don't forget to take your medicine," Harriett said, while pouring coffee and making toast. Their routines were mostly the same each day; get up, eat breakfast, read, and watch television. They enjoyed working jigsaw puzzles and there was usually one spread out on the dining room table. Harriett fed and cared for Frenchie, her small black poodle. She enjoyed taking the dog outside, often bumping into neighbors and sharing conversation.

At 97, Velma had neither the energy nor desire to go out much. Harriett, who was 67, had her bad days, but was able to drive them on trips to the store and church. Both of them enjoyed visiting David, Patricia and their 12 year old son David James Wernert, whom everyone calls young "Davey."

Even though David and Patricia were harsh with Harriett and Velma at times, the women trusted them, and depended on them. The ladies especially loved attending St. Andrew's Episcopal Church in West Toledo. Father Phillip Rapp was such a fine man and gave compelling sermons.

After lunch Harriett heard someone at the front door. The time now was about 12:30 p.m. Harriett called out, "Who's there?"

"It's just me, mom," replied her son David. He had his own

key to the house and said he was there to pick up some tires he had stored in the basement. David was with his friend, Richard Arterberry.

The men went to the basement, and soon after, Harriett heard David yell, "We're leaving now, mom, I'll see you later." Harriett didn't see them leave because she was in the kitchen at the time and Velma was napping.

A few hours later, around 5 p.m., Frenchie started barking – someone was at the front door. Harriett opened the door and saw it was Norma Bliss from their church. Harriett had ordered some Christmas cards from Norma's brother, Elwert Bliss. Elwert had polio and lived with Norma. He sold greeting cards out of their home for Acme Specialty Company, and Norma was delivering the orders.

Harriett opened the door just far enough to accept the cards from Norma because Frenchie was trying to run out the door. "Thank you Norma," Harriett said, pushing Frenchie back inside with the side of her foot. Norma replied, "You're welcome, Harriett; I'll see you in church Sunday."

The evening news just ended at 7 p.m. when Frenchie started barking and running from the living room to the hallway. This hallway leads from the dining room to the front door. Velma was in her bedroom and Harriett was watching television in the living room.

Out of sight from Harriett, a dark figure sat on the stairs in the hallway. As the dog cautiously approached, the person petted and calmed the dog.

"Come here, Frenchie," Harriett said. The figure sitting on the steps shooed the dog back toward the living room. Frenchie ran back into the living room wagging his tail. The dog suddenly turned back toward the hallway and again started barking. Harriett got up and walked to the hallway to investigate.

When the intruder heard Harriett get up, he quietly hurried down the hall, through the dining room to the kitchen, and into the living room behind Harriett.

As Harriett started through the doorway she was struck on

the back of the head with a crowbar. Her 5-foot 110 pound body crashed to the floor while the killer struck her again on the back of the head.

The attacker heard Velma Bush walking toward the kitchen to see what was wrong. She had her flashlight in her hand and as she approached the living room doorway the attacker came up from behind and struck her three or four times on the back of the head with the crowbar.

The blows knocked Velma's 4 foot-8 inch, 90-pound body to the floor. When the killer was sure she was dead, he rolled her over and dragged her into the kitchen by her legs. Velma's wig and flashlight lay near the living room where she was attacked.

The killer was surprised to hear a noise by the front door and went to see what it was. He saw that Harriett had crawled from the living room entrance to the hallway, and now was lying at the base of the front door.

There was a large blood spot and blood splatters on the carpet where Harriett was struck and fell. The killer wanted to make it look as though two murderers had committed the murders, so he went to the basement and found a hammer. He hit Harriett two or three times in the head with the hammer. Blood splatters sprayed the door, walls, and ceiling.

Harriett lay dead at the foot of the front door. The killer sat down on the upstairs steps and played with Frenchie the dog.

The killer took the hammer and crowbar to the basement and opened the valve on the hot water tank, allowing the water to run freely on the floor. The killer sat on a chair washing the blood from the weapons and his hands. The hammer was left on a workbench, but the killer took the crowbar with him. The water was left running in an attempt to wash blood and shoe prints from the floor.

The murderer ransacked the house, stole some jewelry, and took the telephone off the hook in Velma Bush's bedroom, and then fled in Harriett Wernert's red Ford Mustang.

Two defenseless women had been silenced by a cold-blooded murderer. The affluent and serene village of Ottawa Hills would never be the same.

Victims – Harriett Wernert and Velma Bush

Home of Harriett Wernert and Velma Bush
2130 Emkay Drive
Village of Ottawa Hills

3

Discovery Of The Bodies

Bill Relph, an old army buddy of Harriett Wernert's husband James, called Harriett the evening of Nov. 18, from his home in Detroit. Mr. Relph was the president of their army reunion group, and Harriett was still a spouse member. Even though Harriett's husband was deceased and she no longer attended the reunions, Relph still called her occasionally to see how she and her mother were doing.

Relph thought it odd that Harriett didn't answer the telephone – she and her mother Velma were always home in the evening. When he called back a half hour later, the phone was busy. Relph tried two more times, but the busy signal was constant. Finally he gave up, thinking there was trouble on the line.

"Ottawa hills police department," responded police dispatcher Louise Derkis. "My name is David Wernert, and my wife and I are worried about my mother Harriett Wernert and my grandmother Velma Bush. They live at 2130 Emkay Drive and we have been calling them all day, but every time we call we get a busy signal. Please send a police crew to check for their safety."

"Where can I reach you?" the dispatcher inquired. "We are at Tony Packo's restaurant on Front Street in East Toledo with some friends, and we will wait here for your call," David said. It was a little before 8 p.m. on Wednesday, Nov. 19, the night after the murders, when he made the call. He and other members of their racing club were having a meeting at the restaurant.

Tony Packo's is a nationally known Hungarian restaurant that was opened in 1932 by Tony Packo and his wife Rose. It is located in the heart of the Hungarian neighborhood on the east side of Toledo, and is still run by the Packo family. The restaurant is known for its famous Hungarian hot dogs, but also serves tasty hamburgers, stuffed cabbage rolls, chicken paprikas, potato salad, and chili. Packo's famous pickles, peppers, and hot dog sauce, are also sold in grocery stores nationwide.

Tony Packo's gained national fame when Toledo-bred actor Jamie Farr, who played the character Cpl. Max Klinger on the long-running TV series M*A*S*H, mentioned the restaurant in several episodes. Farr played the role of a soldier pretending to be a transvestite in an attempt to get a Section 8 discharge from the Army. The notoriety attracted many famous people to the restaurant, including Hollywood actors and politicians.

In 1972 Burt Reynolds visited Tony Packo's at the request of Nancy Packo, and after eating one of their famous hot dogs, signed a hotdog bun for Tony Jr. A tradition was born with Reynolds' gesture, and since then, when celebrities and dignitaries ate at the restaurant, they signed a hotdog bun. Instead of regular buns, Styrofoam buns are used, and many famous signatures are encased on the walls of the restaurant.

"Units 45 and 87, check for the safety of the occupants at 2130 Emkay Drive."

"Unit 45, OK," responded Sgt. David Anmahian.

"Unit 87?" inquired the dispatcher.

"Unit 87, OK," acknowledged Officer John Nyitray.

Upon arrival at 8:16 p.m. Sgt. Anmahian approached the front door of the house while his partner, Officer Nyitray, went to the back of the house.

Sgt. Anmahian rang the front doorbell, but he received no

response. The front drapes were pulled shut so he could only see part of the room. However, he was able to peer through the small panes of the stained glass door windows and observed a small black dog sitting in the hallway. He saw that the television in the living room was on, and there were lights on.

Sgt. Anmahian walked around to the south side of the house where he noticed the laundry room storm door was closed, but the inside door was ajar. From outside he could see through the laundry room into the kitchen. Using his flashlight he opened the storm door and entered the house. He observed the body of a woman lying on her back in the kitchen next to the kitchen counter. She was lying in a large pool of blood. Her hair, clothing and body were covered in blood. As he got closer he observed no signs of life. He backed out of the house and called for Officer Nyitray to meet him on the south side of the house.

Nyitray had entered the house via the rear screened-in patio porch. He found the door from the porch to the dining room standing open. The door had five window panes and the third pane down was broken. There was masking tape to the right of the broken section. It appeared someone had placed the masking tape on the window to muffle the sound of the breaking glass, and then reached inside and unlocked the deadbolt.

With gun drawn, Nyitray cautiously entered and saw an elderly woman lying on her back in the kitchen with her legs drawn up toward her chest. She was covered in blood.

The officer continued to the hallway and saw another woman lying face down in front of the door. There were gaping wounds to the back of the victim's head and blood splatters on the door, ceiling and walls. A small black poodle was sitting next to his master.

Nyitray slowly retraced his steps back to where he entered the house. Just as he walked out the patio door Sgt. Anmahian radioed him to meet on the south side of the house. "There are two dead ladies in the house and they are covered in blood," Nyitray nervously explained to Anmahian.

"Call for the rescue squad and I'll notify the chief," said Anmahian. Within minutes, Ottawa Hills paramedics Robert Deeds and John Dawley raced to the scene. As the emergency vehicle rolled to a stop, the paramedics grabbed their medical bags and without missing a step entered the house.

"It's too late, John, no pulse," Deeds said. "Call the coroner; there is nothing we can do."

Sgt. Anmahian notified the police dispatcher that the house had been burglarized and they were now investigating a double homicide. "Notify the coroner and crime scene technicians," Anmahian said.

Lucas County Coroner Harry Mignerey and his investigator, Joseph Inman, arrived to examine the bodies. Dr. Mignerey fixed the time of deaths at between 7 and 10 p.m. the night before. He ruled the deaths homicides from blunt force trauma.

Ottawa Hills Police Chief Edward Wechtel notified Ottawa Hills prosecutor Robert Dorrell, Lucas County prosecutors Melvin Resnick and James Bates and the Toledo Police dispatcher. Since the homicides occurred in Lucas County all those people had an interest and assembled at the crime scene.

Toledo Police Sgt. David Roberts and Detective Thomas Ross arrived to offer their assistance, but left after the technicians and Ottawa Hills police took charge.

Edwin Marok, Toledo Police Scientific Investigation Unit technician, arrived along with two Ohio Bureau of Criminal Identification and Investigation technicians, Willian H. Dailey Jr. and James Hockenbery. They processed the scene for forensic evidence, searched for latent fingerprints, collected physical evidence, and took photographs.

Every room in the downstairs had been ransacked with drawers pulled out of dressers, and things thrown around the floors. The upstairs, consisting of two bedrooms, a study, and a storage room, did not appear to have been entered.

Technician Marok made note that the body of Harriett Wernert was found lying face down at the base of the front door. She had penetrating skull wounds on the back of the head and there was blood splattered all about her. Her glasses were at her left side and she was dressed in a robe, nightgown, and slippers.

Marok took photographs, and then proceeded to the kitchen where he photographed the body and area around victim Velma Bush. She was lying on her back and her dress was up around her waist. She too had severe wounds to the back of her head and a cut on her face. There had been extensive bleeding from the wounds. To the left of her body were her smashed glasses and hearing aid. The victim's wig and a flashlight were on the floor of the kitchen near the entrance to the living room.

The technicians found no murder weapons and the only fingerprints were those of the victims and family members. Finger and hand impressions were found throughout the house and in the area of the victims, but with no ridge details. This indicated that the killer wore latex or rubber gloves.

Meanwhile, Ottawa Hills Police Lt. Joseph Eich, Sgt. Anmahian, and Officer Nyitray searched the neighborhood for weapons, evidence, and witnesses.

Nyitray talked to Bruce Friedman of 2119 Emkay. Although Mr. Friedman hadn't seen anything suspicious, he did say that Harriett Wernert owned a red 1970 Ford Mustang. When the house was searched, there was no Mustang in the victims' garage or in the driveway. The only vehicle in the garage was a Triumph racing car owned by David. He stored the car in his mothers' garage because he didn't have room in his garage.

With the help of the Maumee police's computer network, Nyitray was able to track down the serial number and license plate number of the stolen Mustang. A broadcast was put out to other police departments in hopes of catching the killer with the car.

The bodies of Harriett Wernert and Velma Bush were taken to the Medical College Hospital morgue where the autopsies would take place.

After the discovery of the bodies, Toledo Police officers Gene Meyers and Ralph Waniewski were dispatched to Tony Packo's with instructions to take David Wernert to the Ottawa Hills station. Upon their arrival they were met by Ottawa Hills Officers William Snell and Paul Hanslik.

Snell and Hanslik took David Wernert into Chief Wechtel's

office and broke the news of his mother, and his grandmother being bludgeoned to death by an unknown intruder.

"I can't believe this," said David. "I just talked to them yesterday at noon when I went to their house to pick up some tires I stored in their basement."

"Tell us about when you saw them last, and why you called the police to check on their safety," requested Hanslik.

David said he was on his lunch hour from his job as a parts manager for Will Dennis Volkswagen when he stopped by his mother and grandmothers home. The women were fine, and as he left their house he noticed a GT-6 sports car in the neighbors' driveway. The home is owned by Angela Eastman, but she had moved out. The car he noticed belonged to Mark Bellg, who was trimming some trees for the homeowner. David said he belongs to Team Baron racing club with his wife Patricia, and some friends.

He felt the car could be used for racing so he asked Bellg if he would be interested in selling it. Bellg said he hadn't really thought about it. David told him if he decided to sell the car to leave his name and telephone number with his mother, and he would get back with him. "My mother called me later in the day, and told me Mark Bellg called and left his number," David said. This was the last time he talked to his mother.

David advised the officers that both he and his wife made several attempts to call his mother today, but kept getting busy signals. He said his wife works for a veterinarian and was checking with the veterinarian about problems his mother and grandmother were having with their tropical fish. Some of the fish in their tank were dying, and his wife was working with them, and the veterinarian, in an attempt to find out what was wrong with the fish.

Early this evening, he and his wife went to Tony Packo's restaurant for a Team Baron race club meeting. Their son Davey was spending the evening with a friend. Others in attendance at the meeting were Richard Arterberry, Ronald Wyatt, Michael and Joan Stockman, Jan and Dick Dagner, Jan and Don Reed, and Randy and Joanne Carnes. It was around 8 p.m. when he called his mother and grandmother again, but the line was still busy.

They really got worried so he called the Ottawa Hills police and asked the dispatcher to send a crew to their home and check on their safety.

Officer Snell asked David if he knew of anyone who would want to harm his mother and grandmother, or anyone who might break into their home. "No," he replied. "My mother did complain that she kept getting telephone calls from some business, and when she asked them what number they wanted, they would give her number 536-1666. Other than that, there had been nothing suspicious.

Snell and Hanslik were interrupted by David's friend, Richard Arterberry. Arterberry wanted to see what was going on. The officers told him that they could not divulge any information and that he could talk to David when they were finished talking with him. Arterberry left in the same car he came in, a red Porsche.

Patricia Wernert was driven to the Emkay Drive home by their friend Ronald Wyatt, but she was not permitted to enter the house. She was told the house was a crime scene and no one could enter until it had been processed by the crime scene technicians. She was allowed to take Harriett Wernert's poodle home with her.

Lucas County Coroner's Office
November 20, 1975

Prosectors perform the dissection of the body and assist the coroner in determining the cause of death.

The prosectors who assisted with the autopsy of Velma Bush were M. Eltaki, M.D. and Chandnani, M.D. The prosectors who assisted with the autopsy of Harriett Wernert were J. Shin, M.D. and Chandnani, M.D.

After the bodies were prepared, the coroner, Doctor Harry Mignerey, examined them for the cause of death.

Dr. Mignerey ruled that the death of Harriett Wernert was a homicide caused by multiple blows to the back of the head. He reported diffused brain damage with hemorrhage from multiple depressed skull fractures. It appeared that two different weapons were used, a crowbar type and a hammer type.

The coroner ruled that the death of Velma Bush was also a homicide caused by multiple blows to the back of the head. There was diffused subarachnoid hemorrhaging due to left parietal frontal and occipital skull fractures. The wounds were possibly caused by a crowbar or tire iron.

Relatives, friends, neighbors, and village residents exclaimed, "Who would do such a thing?" "They were such sweet, loving, friendly, thoughtful and defenseless people, how could this happen? But, it did happen, and they could only conclude that if it can happen in this quiet village, then it could happen anywhere.

Tony Packo's nationally known Hungarian Restaurant
1902 Front Street, Toledo, Ohio
Photograph taken by Toledo Police Department
Photographer Sgt. Keefe Snyder

Ottawa Hills Police Department
Photographer – Sgt. Keefe Snyder

Edward Lloyd Wechtel
Chief of Police
Village of Ottawa Hills Police Department

4

Search For Witnesses, Evidence, & Murder Weapons

While the crime scene at the victims' house was still being processed by the evidence technicians, and after Harriett Wernert's car had been reported stolen, Westgate Shopping Center Security Guard David Axilrod, made an important discovery.

Axilrod was patrolling the Toledo shopping center grounds when he heard the police broadcast about Harriett Wernert's stolen 1970 Ford Mustang.

Axilrod spotted the stolen car behind the Kroger Store in the shopping center parking lot at 11:09 p.m. He radioed his supervisor, Robert Richards, who notified Ottawa Hills and Toledo police.

Ottawa Hills Officer Hanslik was sent to the scene and verified the car as being the one stolen from the home. Toledo Officer John Zawisza was also dispatched to the scene because the car was recovered in Toledo.

The stolen car was towed to the Ottawa Hills police department garage to be processed.

Technicians William Dailey and James Hockenbery found no fingerprints or evidence of value while processing the car. It appeared that the killer had either worn gloves or wiped the car clean before abandoning it.

A witness, Barbara Cline, had observed the car parked behind Kroger's on her way to work at the shopping center on the night of the murders, but did not see anyone around the car.

"The murders are an isolated incident," said Ottawa Hills Mayor Frank Voss. "We have never had a murder in the village. People reside here because of the low crime rate and serenity of the village; people feel safe here."

"I have all the faith in the world in our chief of police, Edward Wechtel, and the police officers of the village. They do a great job, but it will take people a long time to get over this."

Councilman S. Stewart Cockrang echoed Mayor Voss's praise for Chief Wechtel, and the policemen. "We have a fine police force," he said. "We will be meeting with the chief to evaluate what happened and listen to his recommendations on how to prevent this type of horrible crime from reoccurring."

The chairman of the village council's safety committee, Gunnard Rubini, said he was shocked by the murders because their police patrols are much more concentrated then in large cities. He said the village is only two square miles, so the patrols are in the same areas more often.

The vacant home next door to the victims, belonging to Angela Eastman, was burglarized the week before the murders. The Eastman home was broken into in the same manner as the victims' home, with entry gained by taping the rear door window glass with masking tape, then breaking the window, reaching inside, and unlocking the door. Masking tape was used to muffle the sound of the glass breaking.

Mrs. Eastman had moved out of the home before the burglary, so there was no one home at the time of the burglary.

A neighbor of Mrs. Wernert and Mrs. Bush, Elizabeth Graham, said she was home at the time of the murders, and although she lives only two doors away, she did not see or hear anything. Graham said she has always felt safe, but now is concerned.

Gudelia Rodriguez-Torrez and her husband, Dr. Ramon Torrez, said they had changed all the locks on their doors since the murders. They lived across the street from the victims and knew them well. Mrs. Torrez visited with the ladies and talked with them on the telephone. She said they and other neighbors have always felt safe in the village, but were now fearful.

Another neighbor had her alarm company out testing the system when the serviceman accidentally set off the alarm. She and the serviceman were startled when the police arrived with guns drawn.

Neighbors and residents increased security methods. Deadbolt locks were added, lights were left on at night, and some even purchased guns for protection.

The Ottawa Hills police beefed up patrols and made themselves more visible, but the fear remained.

Pastor Phillip Rapp, assistant rector of St. Andrew's Episcopal Church knew Velma and Harriett well. He said they usually came to church every Sunday and took part in meetings and other church functions.

"They were terrific ladies," he said. "They had many friends in the congregation, and were well liked. Velma did well for her advanced age, but her failing health made it necessary for her to spend time in nursing homes on occasion. "What a shame that Velma and Harriett's lives had to end in such a manner," he said.

In the days to follow and at the direction of Chief Wechtel, Lt. Joseph Eich, Sgt. David Janowiecki, Sgt. David Anmahian, Officers Paul Hanslik, William Snell, and Christian Lopinski searched the neighborhood, creeks, and secluded places in the village for the murder weapon. They used metal detectors but all they found were bottle caps and cans. After days of searching the results were the same, no weapon.

The village offered a $5,000 reward for the arrest and conviction of those responsible for the murders of the two women.

The funerals for Velma Bush and Harriett Wernert were held at Parks D. Emmert Funeral Home. Services were conducted Nov. 22 at St. Andrew's Episcopal Church, and interment was at Ottawa Hills Memorial Park.

Among those in attendance with David, Patricia, and young Davey Wernert, was James Scott Wernert and his wife Deborah. On the pew next to David and Patricia was their good friend Richard Arterberry. With somber expressions they all shared in communion.

St. Andrew's Episcopal Church
Toledo, Ohio
Victim's Church

5
Suspicions

Chief Wechtel said the crime scene led him to believe that there may have been more than one assailant, because the coroner said two weapons were involved and the women were murdered in two different locations in the house. They thought the murders were a burglary gone sour, due to the apparent forced entry, ransacking of the house, and stolen car.

On Thursday, Nov. 20, Lt. Eich called the Toledo Police detective bureau and asked to speak with me. He said he was aware that I had investigated many burglary cases in Toledo and that some were near their jurisdiction. Eich wanted to know if I might be able to give him some names of people who could be responsible for the break-in at the victims' home.

I suggested he first might want to look at the heirs of Velma Bush and Harriett Wernert. Since the victims were wealthy, he should look at the relatives first, to make sure the killer wasn't an heir. He said they felt the evidence indicated the killer or killers were burglars. I told him to check his schedule and call me back with a time we could meet and discuss the case.

It was 11 a.m. on the Saturday after the murders when Chief Wechtel received an all-important telephone call.

"Chief," Don Sugarman here."

"How are you, Don? It's nice to hear from you." Sugarman was a state parole officer and the men had become friends through their professional contacts.

"Chief, I know you are in the middle of a double homicide and I have someone here I want you to talk to. He has some information that I think may be of help to you."

Sugarman handed the telephone to Don Bedra.

Bedra worked part time as a police officer for the Clay Center police department, and full-time as a loss prevention security officer for Rink's Bargain City Stores.

Bedra proceeded to tell the chief what he knew. He was friends with David and Patricia Wernert and Richard Arterberry. He said Arterberry had been staying at the home of the Wernerts on Christie Street in Toledo. He said he met the Wernerts and Arterberry in September 1974 through Team Baron, a racing club they all belonged to.

Bedra said he had been to the Wernerts' home on many occasions and on Sunday, Nov. 16, while visiting, he saw Arterberry with a red 1974 Porsche. Arterberry and the Wernerts all admitted that they had taken part in stealing the car from Will Dennis Volkswagen.

"David Wernert is the parts manager for the auto dealer," he said. They admitted that David Wernert and Arterberry painted the blue Porsche red to disguise the car. Bedra claimed he only knew about the stolen car and had no direct knowledge about the murders of David's mother and grandmother.

After the telephone call, Chief Wechtel felt that if Arterberry and the Wernerts were involved in stealing a car then perhaps they or someone close to them could be involved in the homicides.

Chief Wechtel's department was made up of excellent policemen, but they weren't experienced in handling homicides. There had never been a homicide in the village before, so Chief Wechtel made a command decision to call the Lucas County prosecutor's office for assistance.

He contacted Division Chief Melvin Resnick and assistant

prosecutor James Bates. They were familiar with the case because they had been to the scene of the murders on the night it occurred. During their conversation, Chief Wechtel asked that I be his lead investigator. "Would it be possible to use Frank Stiles?" Wechtel asked. The prosecutors said they would arrange a meeting with me, my supervisors, Capt. Kenneth Rebensal, Deputy Chief Raymond Vetter, and Chief of Police Corrin McGrath.

The meeting was held on Tuesday, Nov. 25 at the Lucas County prosecutor's office. Chief Wechtel described his telephone call from Don Sugarman and Don Bedra. All agreed we could build a good case for the stolen Porsche from Will Dennis Volkwagen, but there was nothing to link anyone to the murders. It was felt that a good interrogator was needed in an attempt to solve the case. Permission was given for me to lead the investigation from that point forward.

Chief Wechtel and I immediately visited the crime scene on Emkay. Fortunately for me, the house had been sealed by the coroner and therefore protected since the night of the homicides. The only thing missing were the bodies of Velma Bush and Harriett Wernert, but with the use of photographs taken by the evidence technicians, I was able to observe exactly where the ladies were found.

I examined the rear door, off the screened-in porch, where the point of entry was thought to have been. I observed the taped and broken door window leading to the dining room. I pointed out to Chief Wechtel that entry to the house was not gained by taping the window, breaking the glass, then reaching inside and unlocking the deadbolt.

The hole in the glass was too small and too far away from the deadbolt for the murderer to have entered by these means. If the glass had been broken while the women were alive, Velma Bush would most likely have heard the glass break. Velma's bedroom was off the dining room and just a short distance from the door.

By examining the photographs, I observed that the door leading from the laundry room, to the south side of the house, was standing open and the screen door was closed. There was no sign of forced entry by this door. The service door leading to the garage was closed and the overhead door was closed. No signs of forced entry were observed. The front door was closed and locked, with the body of Harriett Wernert lying in front of it. There were no signs of forced entry here either.

I advised Chief Wechtel that the murderer either had a key, was let in by the victims, or a door was left unlocked so entry could be made. In other words it looked like an inside job.

The house gave the appearance of a burglary because drawers had been pulled out of dressers and items were strewn around the rooms. The drawers had not been dumped, indicating the killer was trying to make it look like a burglary.

I pointed out that many visible and valuable items - television sets, small amounts of money, credit cards, checkbooks, fur coats, adding machine, typewriter, and other valuables - were left behind by the killer. I said, "Believe me, if burglary would have been the motive, the burglar would not have left those items behind, especially since he stole the victims' car. If the murderer had been a burglar, he would have loaded up the car with all those items and carried them away."

When I examined the area where Harriett Wernert was found, I observed a large blood spot and several small splatter spots on the living room carpet. The photos showed Harriett lying face down in front of the front door with her feet toward the living room.

I told Chief Wechtel that this evidence indicated to me that she was walking from the living room toward the front door when she was struck on the back of the head with the crowbar type weapon the coroner had described in his report. It appeared she laid on the carpet just inside the living room, then crawled a few feet to the base of the front door where she was struck with a hammer, the second weapon the coroner had described. She died at the front door where she was found in a pool of blood.

Next I examined the kitchen area where Velma Bush's body was found. Again, with the use of the photographs, I was able to reconstruct her murder scene. The evidence indicated she was struck on the back of her head multiple times with the crowbar as she started from the kitchen to the living room. In front of the doorway, Velma's wig, flashlight, glasses, and hearing aid were found.

The evidence further indicated she was then rolled over and dragged by her legs back into the kitchen. Her dress was up around her waist, indicating she had been dragged by her legs for this short distance. There was a large pool of blood surrounding her body, which continued to the doorway leading to the living room. We could see drag marks in the blood. Her injuries were caused by just one weapon, most likely a crowbar or tire iron.

I told Chief Wechtel the evidence indicated this was an inside job, and the women were murdered by someone who wanted to make sure they were dead, because they probably knew their killer.

The killer most likely had a key to the house or found a door unlocked. He probably saw Harriett Wernert in the living room while she was watching television, because the TV was found on. The killer must have made some noise and Harriett was walking to the front door hallway to investigate when she was struck. She fell to the carpet and the killer left her for dead. He heard Velma Bush walking from her bedroom to the kitchen. He came up from behind her and struck her. For reason unknown, he rolled her over and dragged her back into the kitchen.

The killer found that Harriett had crawled from the living room to the front door. The only reason I could conclude for using a hammer as his second weapon was to make sure she was now dead and also to make it look like two people were involved in the murders. The killer then went to the basement and opened the water tank valve, washing the blood from his hands and the murder weapons. He left the valve open to allow the water to cleanse the floor of blood and any shoe prints he may have left.

The killer made the crime scene look like burglars had committed the offense by pulling out drawers and taping and breaking the rear door window. He stole jewelry then fled in Harriett's mustang.

I advised the Chief of my theory: only one killer was involved in the murders; the victims knew him, and murder was the motive, not burglary. The murderer was taller than the victims, because the injuries were located on the top of the victims' heads.

While checking the basement for evidence, I found a hammer on a workbench. We took it and some other tools to be tested for blood. Toledo police crime lab supervisor, Sgt. Rick Zielinski, tested the hammer and other tools for blood. He found a small spot of blood on the hammer. The crowbar Harriett Wernert and Velma Bush were bludgeoned with was not found in or around the house.

Chief Wechtel and I had a list of possible suspects provided by witness Don Bedra, and I had my theories. Our work had just begun.

Detective Sgt. Frank P. Stiles
Toledo Police Department

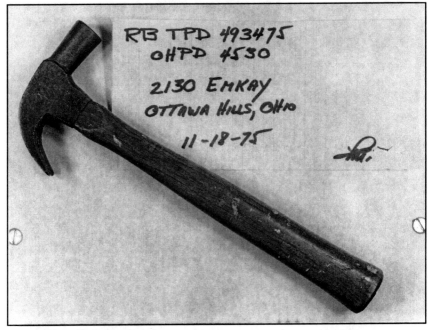

Hammer
One of the weapons used to murder Harriett Wernert

6
Moving Forward

After Chief Wechtel and I examined the crime scene I read the available police reports and evaluated the photographs related to the murders. I also scheduled a meeting with Don Bedra, the witness who knew about the Wernerts and Arterberry stealing the 1974 Porsche from David's employer, Will Dennis Volkswagen.

Wednesday, Nov. 26, 1975

Bedra reiterated what he had told Chief Wechtel earlier, that he was friends with David and Patricia Wernert and Richard Arterberry. "I met then in September 1974 through Team Baron Racing Club," he said.

After a while they began to trust him and talked openly. He repeated what he told Wechtel, that while visiting the Wernerts he watched them working on the red Porsche in their garage. David and Arterberry were buffing the new coat of paint on the car. Patricia was there too, and they all spoke freely about how they stole the car from the dealership where David worked as a manager in the parts department.

The story told was that David gave Arterberry a blank Porsche key he took from work. During business hours the following day Arterberry and Patricia went to the dealership and took the car out for a test drive. While test driving the Porsche, Arterberry had a key made for the car using the blank key David had given him earlier. After the dealership was closed, they went back and stole the car.

Bedra said around this time Patricia Wernert started playing up to him and wanted to have sex. He said she told him that she and David were no longer intimate. Bedra said he turned her down.

In early October, Patricia started telling him things, like being friends with people in the Mafia. He said she asked him if he would be interested in being a "hit man," and asked if he would kill someone for her if she asked him to. She offered to pay him $4,000 to do the job, but when he asked her who she wanted dead, she replied, "You will be told who and when at the time the murder is to take place." He said that after he told her she was crazy, she dropped the subject and never brought it up again.

Arterberry was living with the Wernerts and was driving the stolen Porsche like it was his own. He said Arterberry carried a .38-caliber pistol in the car and indicated that the guy was unpredictable.

According to Bedra, Patricia never actually told him they planned to kill Harriett Wernert and Velma Bush. But Bedra's brother Craig told him that Patricia mentioned she wouldn't mind knocking off the old ladies. His brother said Patricia wanted the women's money so they could use it for their racing club activities.

Bedra also said Patricia Wernert mentioned several times that she hated Harriett Wernert.

I asked Bedra if he could get the serial number and license plate number from the Porsche and he said he would try.

Bedra contacted us later with the serial number, 4742900442, and Ohio license number, M 32444. I confirmed it was the stolen car. The license plate matched Arterberry's recently junked 69 Chevy.

Craig Bedra was also interviewed. He worked for Clay Center Police Chief Roy Miner in Genoa, Ohio. He said he worked there part-time and full-time for Tee Vee Service Club in Toledo. He met the Wernerts and Arterberry through the racing club, and lived with the Wernerts on Christie Street in Toledo in June and July of 1975.

Craig said that on one afternoon Patricia commented that she wouldn't mind knocking off Harriett and Velma. Patricia and David said it would be nice to have their money for the racing club. He said Patricia did most of the talking. Patricia played up to him while he was staying with them, and wanted him to have sex, but he wouldn't. It was soon after this that he moved out and quit going to the Wernerts.

While interviewing the other witnesses we found that another man, Ronald Wyatt, 23, stayed with the Wernerts during the time of the murders.

We felt the murders most likely involved one or both of the Wernerts, Richard Arterberry, and perhaps Ronald Wyatt, but we just didn't know for sure - we needed more evidence.

Record checks showed that neither David Wernert nor his wife had police records. Arterberry was arrested for burglary and auto theft as a juvenile and for carrying a concealed weapon as an adult. Arterberry never did time in jail; he apparently had a good attorney. I found that Ronald Wyatt only had traffic violations and was wanted on a bench warrant for not showing up for court on a speeding charge.

Chief Wechtel and I drove by David and Patricia Wernert's home on Christie Street, and right there in their driveway was the stolen Porsche.

"Look at that, Chief, they're not even trying to hide the car. It's right there in the driveway for anyone to see."

"It's time for me to get the search warrants," I said. "Once we have the warrants we can plan our next move."

We didn't have sufficient evidence to obtain arrest warrants for the murders, but we could obtain search warrants for the home and premises of David and Patricia Wernert, and for the stolen car.

After the search warrants were prepared I presented the affidavits to Toledo Municipal Court Judge Roy Dague, who authorized the warrants.

Meanwhile Chief Wechtel received an unusual telephone call. It was from a woman who said she may have some important information, but that her identity must remain confidential. Chief Wechtel assured her we would honor her wishes and she invited us to her home.

It was 7 p.m. when we arrived. She took us to the basement so we could talk in private; she didn't even want her family to know what she had to say.

"You must never tell anyone about what I am about to tell you," the lady said. She said she had information concerning Richard Arterberry and his former attorney, Arthur James, who had gotten Arterberry out of all the trouble he had been in. She said James felt bad about it because he believed Arterberry may have been involved in the murders of Harriett and Velma.

"Arterberry has been running around with, and staying with Patricia and David Wernert," she said. The visibly shaken woman said the attorney feels that if he hadn't gotten Arterberry out of trouble before he might not now be involved in the murders. She said James didn't know Arterberry was complicit for sure, but had a feeling it was true.

While climbing the basement stairs on our way out of the woman's home, Chief Wechtel and I thanked her for her concern. She was still nervous and shaking when she took my hand and thanked us for coming. I gave her hand a gentle squeeze of assurance and said, "You did the right thing."

1974 Porsche stolen from Will Dennis Volkswagen

7

Making The Right Decision

Armed with the search warrants, Ottawa Hills Chief Edward Wechtel and I set up surveillance on the Wernerts' home.

The time was 10 p.m. on Nov. 26. I had been without sleep for 42 hours by this time. My normal wakeup time was 4 a.m. and after being assigned to assist on the case the day before, I worked straight through.

I tried to get some sleep but the adrenalin wouldn't permit it. I couldn't help but think of the two helpless ladies being bludgeoned to death. We had to move fast and bring the killer or killers to justice. Every good investigator knows you must work fast - the longer the investigation - the less chance you have of solving the crime.

It had started snowing earlier in the evening and it was really coming down now. From our surveillance location we could view the Wernerts' home and garage.

With help of binoculars, we observed David Wernert and Arterberry putting a citizen band radio into the stolen Porsche, parked in the garage. Wernert moved a red Triumph TR6 out of the driveway, and then Arterberry backed the stolen Porsche out of the garage and into the street.

After maneuvering the cars, Wernert and Arterberry entered the house.

Chief Wechtel and I sat in the unmarked detective car, almost mesmerized by the beautiful falling snow and our thoughts on what to do next. We sat there in disbelief of what we had just witnessed. "Now that is good evidence, Chief," I said, smiling. "How lucky is that?"

We saw two of our suspects working on, moving, and driving the stolen Porsche.

We discussed our next move. We had evidence to arrest both Arterberry and David Wernert for possession of the stolen car, but we had little or no evidence to implicate them in the murders of Harriett Wernert and Velma Bush.

I told Chief Wechtel we should get a uniform crew and execute the search warrants. "We could wait until Arterberry leaves in the car and arrest him and hope he admits to the murders, or we can execute the warrants and hope we may find evidence to support the murders."

I radioed the Toledo police dispatcher:

"732 to dispatcher."

"Go ahead, 732."

"Send me a uniform crew to the emergency room parking lot at Toledo Hospital," I directed. "They will be out of service assisting on search warrants."

"OK, 732," responded the dispatcher.

I didn't want to meet the crew near the Wernerts' house for fear they would see the crew and become suspicious. The element of surprise is a tool often used by investigators, and I felt it would take all the tools we had to solve the murders.

The one big advantage detectives have over uniform crews is that a detective has time to plan his strategy, while the uniformed police sometimes have to make split-second decisions based on what they are confronted with at the time.

An investigation of this magnitude requires proper planning - if a wrong move is made, it can blow the whole investigation. All evidence must be evaluated and all suspects examined. In some cases where there is no over abundance of evidence the investigator must rationalize and theorize.

In the case before us, we knew that David and Patricia Wernert and Richard Arterberry had possession of the stolen Porsche, but we were not certain if any of them were actually involved in the murders of Harriett Wernert and Velma Bush.

We had witnesses that said the Wernerts wouldn't mind seeing them dead, but this wasn't proof of murder. We knew Ronald Wyatt, another friend of the Wernerts, was staying with them, and if he wasn't involved, he might have information about the murders. We knew Arterberry had a felony record, but none of his offenses involved violence. Arterberry's former lawyer was suspicious that Arterberry was involved, but this wasn't evidence either. I thought to myself that this was exactly the type of case that required preparation, strategy, and even a little theory.

I felt there wasn't much chance of getting any further evidence as to the murders themselves, unless we saw additional evidence during the execution of the search warrants, or obtained incriminating statements from interviewing the suspects. By what we had learned so far, I felt Richard Arterberry most likely was the murderer who committed the actual killings. I felt David Wernert may reluctantly have been persuaded by his wife to participate.

As for Ronald Wyatt, he may have knowledge of the murders, but I didn't feel he was the actual killer. I knew that a successful conclusion would depend on a beneficial search, followed up by a revealing interrogation

Chief Wechtel and I met Toledo police officers Thomas Medon and William Regan. Toledo Detective James Detrick heard our broadcast to meet the police crew and showed up to offer his assistance.

I advised the officers, that as soon as we entered the house and secured whoever was there, it would be their duty to keep the people in one location, out of the way, while we executed the search warrants.

Our plan was now in place – we surrounded the house and made ourselves known.

8

Execution Of Search Warrants

As the marked and unmarked police cars came to a screeching halt at 2009 Christie St., Officer Regan ran to the rear east corner of the house, covering the back and east side of the house. Officer Medon took the front and west side of the house. Once the house was secured and no one could exit without being seen, Chief Wechtel, Det. Detrick, and I went to the front door of the house.

I rang the doorbell and we were greeted by David Wernert. I advised him that we had warrants for the search of his house, garage, and for the Porsche in his driveway.

As we entered the living room we saw Richard Arterberry on the floor watching TV along with David Wernert's 12-year-old son, Davey. "Is anyone else in the house?" I asked. Wernert said his wife was upstairs taking a bath. I told him to have her get dressed and come downstairs.

I advised all present that we were there to execute search warrants for the house, garage, and Porsche. I gave David a copy of the search warrants and he read them, then passed them to his wife and Arterberry. After they examined the search warrants, I explained their rights.

"Who owns the 1974 red Porsche in the driveway?" I inquired. The Wernerts and Arterberry looked at each other, and there was a moment of silence. Finally, Arterberry said, "I own the car."

"Where did you get the car?" I asked.

"I made it out of spare parts," he said.

"Where are the keys?" I inquired.

Arterberry reached into his pocket and handed me a ring of keys. One of them was for the stolen Porsche. Also on the key ring were two safe depository keys, a handcuff key, a house key, and three small lock-type keys. I told them we had evidence that the car was stolen from Will Dennis Volkswagen. I placed Arterberry under arrest for Grand Theft Auto and had the officers detain him while the search was conducted.

We confiscated clothing and tools with red paint on them. In the garage we found tools, paint cans, brushes, and spray painting equipment. The stolen Porsche was towed to the police garage for evidence.

We found no evidence in the house or garage that implicated anybody in the murders. While looking at a tool box containing tools, I was told that they belonged to Ronald Wyatt.

I told Patricia Wernert to call Wyatt and tell him to come to the house and identify his tools or I would confiscate them. When he arrived I arrested him on the speeding warrant I brought with me.

Arterberry and Wyatt were taken to the police station by officers Medon and Regan with instructions to hold them separately until we were able to interview them.

I advised the Wernerts that they were not under arrest, but that I would like them to go to the police station to answer some questions. They agreed and they and their son Davey rode with Chief Wechtel and me to the police station.

On the way Patricia Wernert said, "We saw in the newspaper that you have been assigned to help solve the murders of David's mother and grandmother. What have you found out?"

I told her I knew the murders were on their minds, but we had to talk about the stolen car first.

At the police station we separated the suspects into different interviewing rooms. I did not want them to have time to talk to each other and prepare alibis.

Chief Wetchel and I decided I would interview the Wernerts and Arterberry. I have always found it better if one person does major interviews. I found that when two people are asking questions the conversation leads in multiple directions and you lose the continuity of the questioning. I prefer to be face to face with the subject so I can watch his expressions and every movement. Body language can sometimes tell an investigator more than words.

I find that by separating suspects, it not only keeps them from building an alibi, but also tends to work on them psychologically. They start thinking, "I wonder what the others are saying. Did they confess to the murders?"

During the more serious investigations I will first interview the suspect without taping his interview with a recorder. If the suspect is cooperative, then I will go over the same questions, but this time I will introduce the tape player. I found if you tell a suspect you are going to tape his interview he is more likely to tell lies, because he knows he is being taped, and he knows the tape is a permanent record he can't dispute. However, I have found once the suspect has told the truth, he is less reluctant to lie during the recorded session. Lying is a way of life with criminals, and they become very good at it.

The tools an investigator has to detect any lies told by the suspect are the facts of the case. If his answers don't compare with what you already know, he is either lying or he did not commit the crime you suspect him of. Another good sign is when the suspect tells two different lies about the same question; therefore it is a good idea to throw the same question at the suspect at different times during the interrogation.

Building a rapport with the suspect at the beginning of the interrogation is a good approach. Prior to questioning, the investigator needs to research the background of the suspect. Find out what types of crime he has committed in the past, what he likes, dislikes, who his friends are, what kind of sports he likes, cars, girlfriends etc. Prior to questioning him about the crime itself, talk to him about himself. Break the ice and many times you will win him over and he will trust you.

I never lie to a suspect; I never promise him anything I can't deliver. An investigator doesn't have much he can offer, but sometimes the suspect might ask to call or see someone close to him after the questioning. If you tell him you will allow this, keep your promise. Many times an investigator will arrest the same suspect over and over again, and if you failed to keep your word in the past, he won't talk to you in the future. Simple things can build rapport and lead to a successful investigation and conviction.

Minimize the crime. If you condemn the suspect and give him no hope, he will not confide in you. I know it is hard to minimize violent crimes such as murder, but an investigator must never show his emotions - the suspect will pick up on this immediately.

I wanted to interrogate each suspect about the stolen car first, so I could strengthen our case on that crime. If I could build a strong case on each of them for the stolen car, then we could at least hold them on that charge, even if they didn't implicate themselves in the murders.

Prior to interrogating Arterberry, and the Wernerts, I sat down for a few minutes to ponder how I was going to conduct the interrogations. An investigator has to be prepared with the known facts and a plan of questioning. If not prepared and confident, the suspect will detect this and clam up. After a few minutes, I was ready to start the questioning.

Toledo Police Department
Safety Building
525 North Erie Street

9
Interrogations

The interviews would take place in rooms near my office on the fourth floor of the Safety Building. Verbal and tape statements were taken from all three.

Thanksgiving morning – Thursday, Nov. 27, 1975, 12:30 a.m.
Interrogation of David E. Wernert for the stolen Porsche

I interviewed the Wernerts and Arterberry separately, starting with David Wernert.

To enhance the probability that the suspects would tell the truth about stealing the Porsche from Will Dennis Volkswagen, I started by telling each of them we had questioned witnesses who stated that the three of them admitted stealing the car and painting it in the garage at the Wernert home. I also told them Chief Wechtel and I had witnessed Wernert and Arterberry working on the car and moving cars in and out of the Wernert garage.

I advised all three that they may as well tell me the truth about the car because being in possession of the stolen vehicle legally carries the same penalty as stealing the car.

To make sure suspects can't claim they were not advised of their legal rights, and didn't knowingly and intelligently waive those rights, I always take certain precautions. I question them about their educational background, and whether they are under the influence of alcohol or drugs. I read them their rights from a waiver form, and then have them read the waiver. I asked them if they understand their rights and if so, are they willing to waive their rights and give a voluntary statement of their own free will? If they acknowledge that they understand my questions, are not under the influence of alcohol or drugs, and are willing to waive their rights and answer questions, I have them sign the waiver. If I later take a tape statement from the suspect, I repeat this policy verbally at the beginning of the tape statement. If the suspect refuses to waive his rights, no statement is taken.

After going over David Wernert's rights with him, and after he waived them, I took his statement.

David stated that he had been employed as Will Dennis Volkswagen parts manager since March 1974. "My wife and I belong to a racing club known as Team Baron, which is associated with a national organization called Fiasco," he said. They belonged to the club with their friend Richard Arterberry and others. "Arterberry has been staying at our house on and off for a few months," he said.

On the morning of Sunday, Nov. 16, Arterberry showed up with the Porsche. He recognized the Porsche as being one from Will Dennis and Arterberry told him that he had stolen the car. "Arterberry wanted to join our club … and said he was going to use the car as his racing car." He said Arterberry told him that his wife, Patricia Wernert, was with him when he took the car for a test drive and when he made an extra key for it, so he could later steal the car.

David said his wife was present when he and Arterberry painted the stolen car red. He said the paint and equipment they used was the same paint and equipment Chief Wechtel and I confiscated from their home and garage with the search warrants.

When I asked David why he helped Arterberry conceal and paint the stolen Porsche in his garage, he said he did it just as a favor to Arterberry.

10

Thanksgiving morning – Thursday, Nov. 27, 1975, 1:10 a.m.
Interrogation of Patricia Wernert for the stolen Porsche

Patricia said that she and David are good friends of Arterberry.

"Arterberry is staying with us and he belongs to our racing club," she continued. "He was interested in getting a Porsche so he could race it with Team Baron."

On Thursday, Nov. 13, she was supposed to meet Arterberry at Will Dennis Volkswagen to test drive different Porsches they had for sale. Before meeting him, she stopped at J.C. Penney's at the Franklin Park Mall. While in the parking lot she bumped into Arterberry and another friend of theirs, Michael Stockman.

Michael worked for Will Dennis as a mechanic. She said they drove up in a black and white Porsche that Arterberry was test driving from the dealership.

Stockman was on his lunch hour and decided to ride along with

Arterberry while he checked the car out. They all had lunch in the mall and then she followed them back to the dealership in her car. Stockman went back to work and she and Arterberry continued test driving different Porsches.

While they were driving a blue Porsche, Arterberry advised her of his intentions to steal the car. He first said he was going to hotwire the car and steal it, but when he found out the car had the kind of ignition that prevented hotwiring; he decided to have a key made for it.

It was late afternoon and Patricia told Arterberry she had to pick Davey up from school. She said they were closer to her home than the car dealer, so she left her Triumph TR6 at the dealership and Arterberry dropped her off at home. Patricia had two cars and said she used her Mercury to pick up Davey. Arterberry said he would pick her up and take her back for the Triumph after he had the key made and after she picked up Davey from school.

A short time later Arterberry picked her up at her house in the blue Porsche. He drove her back to Will Dennis to retrieve her own car. She said before Arterberry dropped her off he told her that he had a key made for the Porsche and intended to steal the car later. She said when they got back to the dealership with the Porsche, Arterberry made a $40 deposit on the car with salesman David Corin. Arterberry had made a deal with the salesman to return in a couple of days to complete the paperwork and make arrangements for the loan.

The next time she saw the Porsche was at her home on the evening of Saturday, Nov. 15. Her husband and Arterberry were painting the car red from its original color of blue. "My husband and I assisted Arterberry in concealing the stolen car because he is a good friend and we felt sorry for him," she said.

Once I finished interrogating David and Patricia Wernert about the Porsche, I arrested them for felony receiving stolen property. I had already arrested Arterberry at the Wernerts' home earlier for the theft of the car, so now all three were in custody.

Chief Wechtel and I made arrangements for the Wernerts' son to be transferred to the Lucas County Children's Home by a police crew until arrangements could be made to place him with relatives or in foster care. Chief Wechtel cared for the boy while the interrogations of his parents took place. We felt bad for young Davey, who had to witness the arrest of his parents. The boy's traumatic experiences had just begun - his life would never be the same.

As for Chief Wechtel and I, the long night continued. I had to interrogate Arterberry for the stolen Porsche, then all three for the murders of Velma Bush and Harriett Wernert.

11

Thanksgiving morning – Thursday, Nov. 27, 1975, 2:20 a.m.
Interrogation of Richard Arterberry for the stolen 1974 Porsche

After Arterberry waived his rights, I confronted him with the evidence against him.

He said he was friends with the Wernerts and was staying with them on and off.

Arterberry and the Wernerts belong to the same racing car club and the Wernerts had their own Triumph racing cars.

"I wanted my own racing car so Patricia Wernert and I planned to meet at Will Dennis Volkswagen to test-drive Porsches. David was the parts manager for the dealership so we knew they had Porsches for sale.

Arterberry confirmed what Patricia Wernert told me, that he and she test drove the blue '74 Porsche, and then he had a key made for the car at Martin Locksmith on Detroit Ave. in south Toledo. He said earlier he and the Wernerts talked about stealing a Porsche from the dealership, and David had given him a blank Porsche key so he could duplicate the key from the Porsche he chose to steal.

Arterberry said he liked the `74 Porsche, so after the test drive, he gave the salesman a $40. deposit to hold the car.

On Saturday, Nov. 15, around 11:30 p.m. David drove him to Will Dennis Volkswagen in a yellow Volkswagen Sirocco two-door car the dealership allows David to use. He used the key he had made earlier to steal the blue 74 Porsche from the car lot. He drove the stolen car to the Wernerts' home on Christie Street and hid it in their garage. He had purchased some red paint earlier from Valley of Paint's paint store on Sylvania Avenue and he and David Wernert used the paint to hide the color of the stolen Porsche.

Arterberry described, while working on the stolen car in the Wernerts' garage on Wednesday, Nov. 26, they installed a citizen band radio and a tape player. He said he purchased the radio and tape player from a customer for $50 about six weeks earlier while he was working as a bartender at Walt's Den Bar in South Toledo.

"The man who sold them to me told me they were stolen, but did not tell me where they were stolen from," he explained. Arterberry said he only knows the man by sight and that he only knows him from coming into the bar on occasion.

The stolen Courier citizen band radio and tape player were in the stolen Porsche when Chief Wechtel and I recovered the car with the search warrants.

Thanksgiving morning – Thursday, Nov. 27, 1975, 3 a.m.
Interview of Ronald Wyatt

After interviewing Arterberry and the Wernerts about the stolen car, Chief Wechtel and I questioned Ronald Wyatt about his relationship with them.

Wyatt said he had been living with the Wernerts since Sept. 12.

Arterberry had just moved in with them about two weeks ago.

Wyatt was aware of the stolen Porsche being at the Wernerts' home on Christie Street and was told by Arterberry and the Wernerts that they had stolen the Porsche, and had painted it. He said they stole the Porsche so Arterberry would have his own racing car.

Wyatt denied any part in the theft of the stolen Porsche and denied any knowledge of the murders of Velma Bush and Harriett Wernert.

I booked Wyatt on an outstanding speeding warrant and he was released pending a hearing. At this time we were not sure if Wyatt was a potential witness for the stolen Porsche case or if he may be involved in the murders or other crimes. I felt I might learn more after I interrogated Arterberry and the Wernerts concerning the murders.

12

Thanksgiven morning – Thursday, Nov. 27, 1975, 6:10 a.m.
Interrogation of Patricia Wernert for the murders

I confronted Patricia Wernert about the murders. I chose to talk with her about the murders first, because I felt she would be the one most likely to cooperate.

When interrogating multiple criminals, the investigator must choose which one to interrogate first. The choice is based on the person's criminal background and personality. This time I found I might have made the wrong choice. Even though Patricia answered my questions and incriminated herself, she appeared to hold back on some things and tried to place most of the blame on her husband and Arterberry.

She stated she was the only child of Alice McCrossen.

"I am 32 years old and I graduated from Monroe High School in Monroe, Mich., on June 10, 1961," she said. Patricia contended she was an average student, receiving mostly Bs and some Cs. She said she and David Wernert were married at St. Andrews Church in Toledo on June 17, 1961, and they had one child, David James Wernert, 12. "My parents divorced when I was 1, and I never knew my real father, George Bloom. My mother remarried Robert McCrossen when I was 6, and they resided in Erie, Mich."

Patricia said she worked for veterinarian Dr. Robert H. Burns at Trilby Animal Hospital on Tremainsville Road as a receptionist. She and her family lived at 2009 Christie St., and the house was owned by David's grandmother, Velma Bush.

Patricia said she had never been in trouble with the police before, a fact I had verified earlier by running a police record check.

The room I was questioning Patricia in was small, and we sat on wooden chairs separated by a small table. My office and the interviewing rooms were located on the fourth floor of the safety building. I was a detective working in the Juvenile Bureau.

I was assigned to the felony section with four other detectives: Bill Case; Larry Prezlawski; Pat Allen; and Dale Siefke. Our job was to investigate felony crimes.

The police department consisting of approximately 250 officers moved into the Safety Building in 1925 from its prior location at 20 Superior Street. In 1975 the department of 725 officers used up much of the five-story building and basement for its bureau of identification and records section, crime laboratory, various sections of the detective bureau, traffic bureau, property room, and administrative offices.

In addition, Toledo Municipal Court was located on the first floor of the building. Only misdemeanor criminal cases and preliminary hearings were heard there; felony cases were tried across the street in Lucas County Common Pleas Court.

In 1975 the police division and the city of Toledo housed and managed its own men's and women's jails. The men's jail was located on the fifth floor of the building and the women's jail took up one half of the fourth floor, where the juvenile bureau and my office were located.

Our offices were small and the interviewing rooms even smaller. I preferred the small interviewing rooms because they were plain, furnished with only wooden chairs and a small table. There were no distractions and the person being interviewed sat across the table just a few feet from the interviewer.

The short distance allowed me to view every movement made by the person being interviewed, and to evaluate every word they spoke. Even though the rooms were small and the offices over crowded, they weren't intimidating or oppressive to the persons being interviewed. After all, we interviewed victims and witnesses in those same rooms.

I always treated everyone courteously unless their actions demanded less. They were offered water, coffee, soft drinks, and even food if the interview went on for a long period. They were provided restroom facilities and the use of a telephone.

On this night – and early morning - while I interviewed each suspect individually, Chief Wechtel passed the time with the others, taking care of their needs. He also made sure they did not converse with each other about the crimes. If they would ask questions, he would tell them I would answer those questions when it was their turn to be interviewed.

Many attorneys look to suppress a client's statement or confession with reasons such as intimidating the suspect, denying them food, drink, use of restrooms, and telephones, and by denying them access to an attorney. The law provides that police furnish some of those privileges and I take precautions to abide by the rules. Not only do I want to follow the law, I feel everyone deserves fair treatment.

In this investigation, I felt that if anyone had a disadvantage and was under pressure and duress, it was me. I was attempting to question four suspects in a double homicide and auto theft. I had not eaten in hours, and I had been without sleep for 45 hours.

As I started my interrogation of Patricia Wernert, I could tell she was anxious and ready to see what I knew. Most suspects will talk to the investigator to see whether they suspect them.

"You know Patricia; I am not just interested in the `74 Porsche you and your husband helped Richard Arterberry steal. I know you are involved in the murders of Velma Bush and Harriett Wernert. You are aware that I have been talking to Arterberry and your husband, and now I want you to be honest with me and tell me the truth about the murders."

Patricia looked at me with an expression of guilt, and then said, "It all started out as a joke, Mr. Stiles. My husband, Richard Arterberry and I started talking about it around Halloween of this year."

She said the three of them thought that it would be a good idea to break into the home of Harriett and Velma, just to shake up the ladies in an attempt to get them to move. David felt the house was too big for them, but they didn't want to move. David also talked about moving to California. "The inheritance did cross our minds, but was not the main reason," Patricia continued.

She said, "We first discussed having Richard Arterberry break into the house on Emkay by using a key that is kept in a jar in the storage shed, adjacent to the house."

Patricia admitted she did not get along with Harriett and said they just tolerated each other, but she loved Velma. "I felt Harriett did not like our son, and really wanted a granddaughter instead of a grandson," she said.

"We did have a little girl, but the baby died and we buried her in Georgia, leaving us with just our son Davey. We were living in Georgia at that time, because David was stationed there while in the Army."

"When we first started talking about the break-in and murders, it was kind of a joke, and we even kidded about having a real body in the coffin for Halloween. On Halloween we often had a coffin with a live person in it for display. At a prearranged time I would signal the person in the coffin and the person would rise up and scare everyone. At first we were joking about the murders, but as the discussions continued they became more serious."

On Tuesday, Nov. 18, she went to work at the Trilby Animal Hospital, as she did every day. When she came home for lunch at noon, her husband and Arterberry were there. During lunch they made their final plans for Arterberry to break into David's mother's and grandmother's house. They talked about Arterberry tying up the ladies and then make it look like burglars committed the offense. "Arterberry was to make it look like a robbery - they were doing this to scare the ladies into moving," she said.

Patricia said the house next door to Velma and Harriett had been broken into recently, indicating the police would think the crimes were committed by the same burglars. The home next door was owned by the Eastman family, but they had moved out prior to their break-in.

The plan was for Richard to go to the home on Emkay around 7pm and get the key from the outside shed adjacent to the house. Patricia said Velma and Harriett prepared for bed around this time – she knew this because she had stayed overnight with Velma one time when Harriett was out of town.

Patricia said, "I don't remember telling Arterberry to take any money or anything, but I was aware the ladies kept approximately $200 in cash in the house. David, our son, and I had a prearranged alibi to be eating dinner at Kings Cove restaurant in Temperance, Mich., with my employer, Dr. Robert Burns, and his wife Donna. Our son Davey was going to babysit the Burns' daughter while we went to dinner."

Patricia said that after finalizing the plans, she went back to work. On the way home from work she stopped by the cleaners and the bowling alley where young Davey bowled.

"Around 6:30 p.m., David and I, and our son drove to Robert and Donna Burns home in Temperance, Michigan," she said. While their son babysat the Burns daughter, the four of them drove to Kings Cove restaurant on Stearns Road. "I drove us there in our car," Patricia said. "After dinner we drove back to the Burns' home and by this time it was around 10 p.m. Soon after, we left the Burns' home and headed for our house. On the way home we stopped at the store to get a few groceries, and then continued home."

She said Arterberry was at their house when they arrived home. He had a dazed look on his face. They asked him what happened and he just stated, "Everything was taken care of."

"What was Richard Arterberry wearing?" I inquired.

Patricia said he was wearing blue jeans and brown zippered boots. "I don't recall what shirt he had on," she said. I asked if he had any blood on his clothing and she said she didn't notice any.

She continued, "On Wednesday I got up and went to work. We didn't get a chance to talk about it after I got off work, and around 7 p.m. that night, David and I, and Richard, went to Tony Packo's." She said they were having their monthly racing team meeting with several other members. Before going to the meeting they dropped their son off at a friend's home for the evening.

Patricia said she called Harriett and Velma's house several times earlier in the day from work, and again from Tony Packo's, but each time she got a busy signal. The last call still had a busy signal so she asked David what had happened. Arterberry said, "They are dead." Patricia said this was the first she knew that Harriett and Velma had been killed. She told her husband to call the Ottawa Hills police and asked them to check on the women.

It was around 9pm when the barmaid at Packo's approached Patricia and David at the bar. The barmaid told them there had been a death in the family and that Toledo police wanted to talk to David in the restaurant office. "David left with the police and when I found this out, my friend Ronald Wyatt took me to the home of Harriett and Velma," Patricia said.

At the home Patricia was met by the coroner, Dr. Harry Mignerey, and Ottawa Hills Lt. Joseph Eich. She was told she could not enter because it was a crime scene. The dog warden was there and was preparing to take Harriett's poodle to the dog pound. Patricia was given permission to take the dog with her.

After they left, Patricia met her husband and Arterberry at the Ottawa Hills police department. Police notified David's brother, James Wernert, of the deaths. The brother resided in California, but said he would come to their home soon. Patricia said after talking to James, they took the dog to the Trilby Animal Hospital for kenneling.

No one was there at the time, but she called her employer and got his permission. Patricia had a key to the hospital because she worked there.

"When we got back to our house I again asked David and Richard what happened to Harriett and Velma; they told me to shut up about it, and they would tell me about it later."

On Thursday, Nov. 20, she did not go to work. Friends were at the house, along with some employees from where David worked. During the day she picked out caskets and got together with an attorney, Arthur James, and they went to the Ottawa Hills police station. With a police officer's permission and in his company, they went to the Emkay home where she picked out clothing to be worn by Velma and Harriett for the funerals.

She said that while alone with Arterberry, she asked him what happened after he broke into the home. Arterberry told her Harriett went to the front door and he thought she was going to turn the light on, so he hit her. He said he heard Velma in the kitchen and thought she was going to the telephone, so he hit her. He did not tell Patricia what he struck the women with.

Patricia said she asked why he had to hurt Velma, because she was old and harmless. Arterberry told her he thought she was going to the telephone and was afraid she was going to call the police. Patricia said, "Things just did not go the way they were supposed to."

People were coming and going all day so she did not get a chance to go into detail, nor talk to him any further then.

"On Friday, Patricia said, "The funeral services were held at Parks D. Emmert Funeral Home at 9 a.m. When we returned home from the funeral, I again attempted to talk to Richard and David about the murders, but had trouble doing so, because David's brother James and his wife Deborah were staying with us."

"Who are the heirs to Velma Bush and Harriett Wernert's estate?" I asked.

"My husband David and his brother James are the heirs," Patricia said.

"How much are their estates worth?" I inquired.

"Velma's estate is worth approximately $400,000, but I don't know what Harriett's is," Patricia responded.

"Why did Arterberry agree to kill Velma and Harriett for you? Was it for money?"

Patricia stated there were no real promises made to Arterberry, but he and David discussed going into business together, and talked about opening a bar in Luna Pier, Mich. Arterberry also mentioned opening a junkyard in south Toledo. She conceded Arterberry may have committed the murders thinking that they would help him go into some type of business.

"Isn't it true, Patricia, that you hated Harriett Wernert, and you told Richard Arterberry to kill her after he broke into the house?"

"I did dislike Harriett, but I loved Velma, and I might have told Arterberry that it would be all right to throw Harriett down the basement stairs, but not to hurt Velma."

"Did you or your husband tell Arterberry to steal something from the house so the crime would look like a burglary?"

She said the women kept about $200 in cash in the house, but she never told Arterberry to steal the money or anything else. She said she never told him, "Steal what you want and keep it for yourself," but she did not know all the things her husband told him.

"Didn't you want the women dead so you and your husband could collect the inheritance?" I asked.

"It might have crossed our minds, but that wasn't the main reason we did it. They were always complaining about their health and Harriett didn't like me or Davey," she said.

13

Thanksgiving morning – Thursday Nov, 27, 1975, 7:20 a.m.
Interrogation of David Wernert for the murders

David stated he was 37, born on Oct. 4, 1938. "I reside with my wife Patricia and our son, David James Wernert, at 2009 Christie St. in Toledo," he said.

"The home is owned by my grandmother, Velma Bush. My wife and I were married at St. Andrew's Church in Toledo on June 17, 1961, and our son, Davey, is 12. I attended DeVilbiss High School in Toledo, but graduated from Ottawa Hills High School in 1956. My formal education was from the University of Toledo and I graduated in 1960 with a business degree."

Wernert said he was employed by Will Dennis Volkswagen as manager of the parts department. He had been employed since March 1974. He owned a `74 Mercury and a Triumph racing car. His father James died in 1972 and he has an adopted brother, James Scott Wernert, married to Deborah, in San Bernardino, Calif.

Wernert's confession was one of the most comprehensive and incriminating confessions I have ever taken. He included all the elements of murder for hire, and for premeditated aggravated murder. I viewed him as a cold, calculating, unfeeling, murderer. I saw his wife and their accomplice, Arterberry, in the same manner. Even though it was Arterberry who bludgeoned Velma Bush and Harriett Wernert with a crowbar and hammer, it was as if David Wernert and his wife Patricia were the ones guiding his hand.

Wernert said he, his wife, and Arterberry had been planning the murders of his mother, and his grandmother, since the end of October 1975.

He contended that his reasons for killing the women were because they were ill, and had been complaining about being in pain. The complaints started as soon as he came home from Vietnam and military service in 1969.

"They complained about their aches and pains and this was a constant worry and pressure on my mind," he said. "My father died of cancer in 1972, and even though my father and I weren't close, this was of great concern, and my mother and grandmother became more of a burden. My brother James in California was no help, although I don't blame him. The burden just became much heavier on me and my wife."

Wernert said the plan to kill his mother and grandmother was discussed very seriously among his wife, Arterberry, and himself at their home, on Monday, Nov. 17. The plan was for Arterberry and him to go to the women's home on the pretense of getting some tires he had stored in their basement.

"We all belonged to a race club called Team Baron and I kept my Triumph in their garage and the tires and equipment in their basement," he said. The plan was for him to take Arterberry to the home on Nov. 18, during his lunch hour, where he could hide in the basement.

Arterberry was to hide until 7 p.m., after he and Patricia had an airtight alibi. The alibi would be eating dinner with his wife's employer, veterinarian Robert Burns and his wife Donna. The Burns family lived in Temperance, Mich., and the Wernerts would be at their house around 7 p.m.

They planned to eat at Kings Cove restaurant on Sterns Road in Temperance. Their son Davey was to babysit the Burns' daughter while they went out to eat. He said this was a prearranged alibi.

While he and his wife were with the Burns, Arterberry was to come up from the basement and take care of the job. When the women were dead, he would put tape on the back door window and break the glass to make it look like a break-in had occurred.

After the murders, Arterberry was to flee the house in Harriett's car.

Wernert said that before hiding Arterberry in the basement, the plan was for him to follow Arterberry to the Westgate Shopping Center on Secor where he would park the Porsche they had stolen earlier. Arterberry was to exchange the cars after stealing his mothers' car.

David said the scheme went as planned - he went to work on Nov. 18 at 8 a.m., then drove to his house at noon to meet his wife and Arterberry. He said the three of them went over the murder plan, then his wife went back to work at Trilby Animal Hospital. David followed Arterberry to the rear of the Kroger store in his car while Arterberry drove the stolen Porsche. He then took Arterberry to Emkay. He went back to work, and later that night he and his wife went to dinner at Kings Cove restaurant with Dr. Burns and his wife as planned.

"After we ate dinner, we went back to the Burns home to pick up Davey. Patricia, Davey, and I left around 10 p.m. We stopped at Food Town to get some groceries and arrived home at approximately 11 p.m. Arterberry was there when we arrived."

Wernert said he did not see any blood on Arterberry's clothing, and when he asked Arterberry what happened, Arterberry gave the following story:

Arterberry remained in the basement until around 7 p.m. when he went upstairs. Wernert said he had given Arterberry a crowbar. He said it was approximately 20 inches long, with a hook on the end.

Arterberry told him and Patricia that he hit Harriett Wernert with the crowbar, and then heard Velma Bush going to the kitchen from her bedroom and hit her too. He hit one of the women with one end of the crowbar, and the other with the other end.

"Did you or your wife tell Arterberry to take money from the house to make it look like a burglary had been committed?" I asked.

He said he didn't recall telling him to take anything, but Arterberry said he ransacked the house, took $11 in cash, some pearls, and a watch. He told them he followed the plan and made it look like a burglary by putting tape on the back door window glass and breaking the window. Wernert said the vacant house next door had been broken into the same way and they felt the police would think the same burglars committed both crimes.

Arterberry said he fled the house in my mothers Mustang and drove to the rear of the Kroger store at Westgate Shopping Center. He exchanged the Mustang for the Porsche. Arterberry said the reality of it all was setting in as he raced from the parking lot.

"How did Arterberry get the keys to your mother's car? What did he say he did with the money and jewelry he stole from your mother and grandmother's home?"

"Arterberry had been to their house with me in the past." Wernert said. He said Arterberry knew where mom kept her car keys; she kept them on the kitchen counter with her purse." Wernert said Arterberry kept the small amount of money he stole, but gave the jewelry to his wife Patricia. He said on Wednesday night, Nov. 26, he and his wife went to the Trilby Animal Hospital, where Patricia was employed. "Patricia had a key to the hospital because she works there," he said.

Wernert said he and his wife entered the animal hospital on Tremainsville Road with his wife's key. "No one was there when we entered; the only sounds came from the barking dogs locked in nearby kennels," he said. His wife had placed the assorted jewelry in a red glass Avon jar. "I took the jar and dropped down through a trapdoor leading into a crawl space under the dog kennels. It was a dirt crawl space with a clearance of about three feet. I crawled for several feet along a block wall to an opening leading to another section under the kennels. There, I buried the jar and jewelry in the dirt, about three inches below the surface," Wernert explained.

I had Wernert draw me a map of where he hid the stolen goods.

I not only wanted to recover the jewelry, but the map would help corroborate his confession. A confession by itself is not sufficient evidence to convict; an investigator needs corroborating evidence to validate the confession. I knew that supporting evidence would be needed, and I searched for it based on the truthfulness of the murderers' confessions. Only the truth can solve cases. Criminal cases are like a jigsaw puzzle: The pieces either fit or they don't fit.

There are basic types of evidence used to solve criminal cases. Testimony of witnesses, experts, and police make up a big part of criminal cases. Physical evidence is tangible evidence found at crime scenes, or gathered during an investigation. Circumstantial evidence is not gained by personal knowledge or personal observations, but rather drawn by association and inferences.

During the investigation of the 1975 murders, investigators didn't have the tools of forensic DNA and automated computer fingerprint comparison.

Deoxyribonucleic acid (DNA), like fingerprints, is a tangible and reliable tool. Experts, including, but not limited to, State and Federal scientist and laboratory technicians, tell us that no two persons have the same fingerprints and except for identical twins, no two people have the same DNA.

A person's DNA can be traced to their biological parents and siblings, but with the exception of identical twins, the DNA is not identical. DNA traced to biological family members is referred to as "Mitochondrial DNA." It may be the next best thing to conclusive individual DNA because it can be traced directly to the person's biological family members when the original donor is not available for comparison.

Criminal identifications have been greatly enhanced in recent years with the used of automated computer fingerprint comparison. Before its development, a latent fingerprint found at a crime scene was of no use unless there was a known suspect. The print lay dormant until a suspect was located and his print compared and matched with the one found at the crime scene. In many cases, a suspect was never developed, so the case went unsolved.

With automated computer fingerprint comparison, local, state, and federal crime laboratories can enter unknown prints into the system to be compared with prior convicted and incarcerated criminals' prints. If the print from the crime scene matches the print of a present or past incarcerated criminal, an immediate identification can be made.

DNA evidence is now entered into a similar database system, and the identification of criminals can be made in the same manner. Both systems are also used to locate missing persons whose fingerprints and or DNA is on file.

DNA was not introduced as a tool for criminal investigations until the mid/late 1980s by Scotland Yard, and then in the United States in the early 90s. In prior years, investigators had to rely on physical evidence from the crime scene, circumstantial evidence gathered from non-conclusive evidence, and from victims, witnesses, and suspects interviewed. DNA and automated fingerprint comparison have become tremendous tools for the police, but have not altogether replaced good everyday police work.

Investigators still must diligently investigate crime scenes and gather evidence, interview victims, witnesses, and suspects. DNA is not always conclusive; many times DNA evidence can be explained away by the donor. There are times the donor has an alibi for his DNA being left at a crime scene. It doesn't mean he is still not a good suspect, and this is where the other forms of evidence can assist in solving the crime.

After Wernert drew me the map of where he had hidden the stolen jewelry, we continued our conversation.

"Who are the beneficiaries of your mother and grandmother?" I asked.

"Me and my brother (James Wernert)," David replied. In response to my next question, he said their combined estates were worth $500,000 to $600,000.

"Did you have them murdered by Arterberry so you could collect the money and property from their estates?" I asked.

"Not really, they always gave us money when we needed it," he said. "The main reason for the murders was to put them out of their misery," he claimed. "They were getting old and were always complaining about their age and health."

"What did you promise Richard Arterberry for killing your mother and grandmother?" I asked.

"I really didn't promise him anything," he said. Arterberry had approached him with some business propositions, but he didn't think the businesses he had in mind were to his advantage, or very practical, and did not give them serious thought.

"Why do you think Arterberry agreed to kill the ladies, if not for money?"

"I think Arterberry killed my mother and grandmother for a new experience and the excitement of it. Richard has been involved in many kinds of things in his young life, and I feel this was a new challenge for him, and I feel this was the actual reason he committed the murders for me and my wife," David said.

I had been given many reasons from criminals about why they committed heinous crimes, but Wernert's explanation and reasoning for the murders of his mother and grandmother at the hands of Richard Arterberry was bizarre, and beyond my comprehension.

14

Thanksgiving morning – Thursday, Nov. 27, 1975, 9:42 a.m.
Verbal Interrogation of Richard Wayne Arterberry for the murders

In response to my questions about his personal background, Arterberry stated he was 21 years old and that his birthday is June 28. Until recently he resided with his mother, Shirley Rose, and stepfather Herbert Rose, at 4528 Satinwood in Toledo. He said he has been staying with Patricia and David Wernert on Christie Street. "My biological father is Richard Lemon Arterberry and he resides at 5002 Clara Street in Alton, Illinois," he said.

Arterberry was born in Illinois but graduated from Sylvania High School in 1972. Even though he and his parents claim he had an IQ of 160 he didn't apply his intelligence to getting good grades. He said he received average grades in school – his grades were extremely good or extremely poor. He was married for a short time to Vickie Ross but they divorced and she moved to Baltimore, Md. "We had no children," he said.

Arterberry said he was presently unemployed but used to work for Jerry Porter Television Repair on Broadway in Toledo. "I am good with electricity," he said. Again, Arterberry told me he also was a bartender for a short time at Walt's Den Tavern in South Toledo. The bar owner was Walter Staerker, and although he wasn't staying there at the time, he rented an apartment from Staerker on Summit Street.

Arterberry said he received a large amount of money through an inheritance some time ago and used the money to buy part ownership in A & A Salvage Company. The business was a body shop and junkyard on Whittier Street. He said the business partnership didn't work out and he lost his money.

"I owned a `69 Chevy, but I junked it recently," he said. "I don't own a car at this time." Arterberry said he bought license plates for the Chevy on Nov. 12, but he only bought the plates so he could use them on the `74 Porsche he stole from Will Dennis Volkswagen.

Arterberry said he has been arrested as a juvenile and as an adult for crimes of breaking and entering, auto theft, carrying a concealed weapon, and various traffic offenses.

When talking with Richard's father, Richard Lemon Arterberry, he told me his son moved to Toledo with his mother, Shirley, after their divorce in 1960. He said he has since been remarried to his wife Maggie. Richard's mother also remarried, to Herbert Rose.

The elder Arterberry said that around 1971, his mother died. She left his son a little over $20,000, but his son could not use the money until he turned 21. He said he was the trustee of his son's money until then. "I gave the money to my son around his birthday, in June of 1975," he said.

The elder Arterberry said that just before his son was arrested for the murders, young Richard came back to Illinois and broke into his house. The neighbors saw him and called police. His son was arrested, but the charges were later dropped.

As a result of my background research of Arterberry, prior to his arrest, I knew he had been jailed several times in the past, but had never admitted his guilt. Even though some of those charges were felonies, he never did any hard time.

After I questioned young Richard Arterberry about his background, I confronted him with the murders of Harriett Wernert and Velma Bush.

It was obvious to me that Arterberry might be reluctant to confess to the murders. He had admitted to the theft of the Porsche earlier, but in that case the evidence was overwhelming. Chief Wechtel and I had witnessed him with the car at the Wernerts' house, and he admitted the car was his. Both Patricia Wernert and David Wernert had implicated him in the theft of the car, so with all this evidence there was not much Arterberry could say or do to escape that charge.

The aggravated murders of Velma Bush and Harriett Wernert were much more serious; Arterberry could be given the death penalty if convicted.

When interrogating criminals, you have to plan your strategy and prepare your form of questioning. Arterberry wasn't reluctant to talk to me, and he never asked for a lawyer. He always waived his rights, but I felt he did this because he wanted to find out what I might know. Even with all his cooperation, I knew that getting him to admit to a double homicide would be difficult.

What could I say to get Arterberry to admit murdering the women? Then it came to me. "I'll use his 160 IQ. I'll let him outsmart himself."

I engaged small talk to get Arterberry to relax, and to build a rapport with him. After I felt I gained his confidence, I told him of the strong evidence I had against him concerning the murders.

"David and Patricia have both given taped confessions as to their part in the killings, and both of them have implicated you as the actual person who murdered the women. David left you in the ladies' basement prior to the murders being committed and you murdered them at 7 pm, the precise time David and Patricia were establishing their alibi while eating dinner with Patricia's employer, Dr. Robert Burns and his wife, at King Cove restaurant.

We can prove you were living with the Wernerts at the time of the murders, and that all three of you stole the Porsche so you could use it for racing with your club. We know you used the Porsche as your getaway car after you committed the murders. We have proof you were with the Wernerts before and after the murders, and that only they created an alibi for the time of the murders. You have no alibi.

"Look, Richard, I don't need you to confess to the murders, I can prove that, but I have to admit you are extremely smart and had me fooled. Just tell me how you so cleverly killed each woman and made it look like more than one person was involved. Where did you get the idea to make it look like burglars committed the murders?"

I could see his ego taking over, and an expression of pride come over his face. I knew I had him; he couldn't wait to tell me how smart he was and how he was able to outwit me at first. I just sat back and relaxed while Arterberry answered all my incriminating questions.

"I met David and Patricia Wernert about two years ago through an automobile racing club we belong to," Arterberry said. "We were only casual acquaintances. "About six weeks before Halloween, I saw them at another club meeting, and after that I started going over to their home on Christie Street because I felt they were extremely nice people to be around."

"What relation were Harriett Wernert and Velma Bush to David and Patricia Wernert?' I inquired.

"Harriett was David's mother and Velma was his grandmother." Arterberry said he has been to the home of David's mother and grandmother on several occasions, and he knew the women. "David kept his Triumph racing car in their garage, and tires and other equipment in their basement," he said.

Arterberry said Patricia and David began talking to him about murdering Harriett and Velma. "I feel I was singled out by David and Patricia for the job of killing them, but I knew they had approached others before me," he said. A friend of theirs, Craig Bedra, told him Patricia and David had approached him while he was living with them, but apparently he wasn't the right man for the job. Craig said he didn't want any part of it, and he quit going to their home.

"Another friend, Ronald Wyatt, was staying with Patricia and David at the time of the murders, and even though he did not admit it to me, I felt the Wernerts had approached him about killing the women. Wyatt didn't kill them, so apparently he was not the right man for the job."

Arterberry started hanging around the Wernerts' home on a regular basis and they kept talking to him about killing the women. He said he found this interesting, and that is the reason he kept going to their house. "I wanted to see how far they would go with it," he said. "I felt Patricia Wernert was testing me to see if I had the courage to do the murders, because a couple of months before the murders she had me steal a `69 Plymouth car from Glass City Dodge on Alexis Road."

Arterberry said Patricia encouraged him to steal the car, and one night she drove him and Ronald Wyatt to the area of Glass City Dodge in her Mercury. He said Wyatt had blown the engine in his `69 Plymouth and they were going to steal another `69 Plymouth so they could use the engine to repair Wyatt's car.

"When we got there, Patricia parked in a car wash next to the car lot. Patricia and Ronald stayed in Patricia's car while I hotwired the car we chose to steal from Glass City Dodge. The car I stole was a two door green `69 Plymouth Roadrunner. We took the stolen car to our friend Craig Bedra's home on Prouty Street in south Toledo and stored it there for awhile.

Craig didn't know we stole the car. Later Wyatt and I took the car to A & A Salvage junkyard on Whittier Street. I used to be partners with the owner there, and a man who works there used their tow truck to help us remove the engine from the stolen car. The man didn't know the car was stolen. Wyatt later put the stolen engine into his own car, and I junked the stolen car at Kasle Iron & Metal Company on Lagrange Street."

Arterberry felt he had passed the test by stealing the car because they actually planned the murders for Halloween night. "I was threatened by Patricia and David and told that if I screwed up I would be taken care of and dealt with," he said. Patricia claimed to have ties with the Mafia, and she also professed to be a witch who could cast spells on people. They were fun to be around, but they were also somewhat scary.

He said Patricia even lied to him and said she had cancer. She told him she was going to die and wanted David to get the inheritance from the old ladies so she could have one last good time before she died. "She tried every angle to get me to murder the old ladies," he said.

"No money was promised to me to commit the murders," Arterberry said. "David and Patricia told me Harriett and Velma were old, sickly, and in pain, so I would actually be doing them a favor by killing them, and putting them out of their misery," he continued.

Arterberry said even though Patricia and David never mentioned giving him money for killing Harriett and Velma, he and David had talked about going into business together. "I felt I would be taken care of after I did the killings, although nothing definite was mentioned to me," he said.

"How much were Harriett Wernert and Velma Bush worth?" I inquired.

"Patricia and David told me they were worth anywhere from a million on down," he said.

Arterberry said he felt the Wernerts' reason for murdering Harriett and Velma was a sick rationalization of the whole thing, and that he could see that now, but not at the time.

Richard, I said, "tell about how the murders were planned and how you murdered Velma Bush and Harriett Wernert."

Arterberry said the Wernerts and he planned the murders at the Wernerts' home. He said David showed up at the house in the Will Dennis Volkswagen company van. "We finalized the murder plan during lunch on Tuesday, Nov. 18."

He said they hadn't stolen the Porsche from Will Dennis for the purpose of a getaway car, but it turned out that way.

"Patricia worked for Trilby Animal Hospital, and she gave me a pair of green colored surgical gloves from the hospital to wear when I committed the murders. Later, during the murders, I wore those and I also wore my own leather gloves on top of the surgical gloves.

During lunch we talked about the murders and how they would be carried out. Our plan was for David to follow me to the rear of the Kroger store in the Westgate Shopping Center. I was to park the Porsche there and then David would drive me to Harriett and Velma's home.

We would enter the old ladies' house on the pretense of getting some tires from the basement. I had been to the home before with David, and Harriett and Velma knew me, so there was no reason they would suspect anything was wrong. The plan was for me to hide in the basement when David went back to work."

Arterberry said David and Patricia had a prearranged alibi to be eating dinner at a restaurant in Temperance, Michigan with Patricia's employer. The plan was for them to be eating dinner at 7 p.m., the same time he was to emerge from the basement and murder Harriett and Velma.

"Now that the plan was in place, Patricia went back to work and David and I left the Wernerts house in our separate vehicles," he said.

"After David and I left the stolen Porsche behind the Kroger Store, we drove to the Emkay house in David's company van. We entered the house through the front door, finding both Harriett and Velma there. David told the women he was going to pick up some tires in the basement.

David left the house while I stayed hidden in the basement. Earlier at Patricia and David's home, David gave me a Craftsman gray crowbar, about 18 inches long, with a hook on one end and straight on the other. It was a wrecking bar type tool. The tool was to be used to make it look like a burglary had occurred, but it ended up being the murder weapon."

"David left me in the basement and I stayed there hiding and waiting for 7 p.m. to arrive. I was waiting until 7 p.m. so David and Patricia Wernert could establish their alibi. I took some Valium that Patricia gave me earlier. I stretched out on the basement floor and fell asleep."

Arterberry said he woke up and heard the evening news on the upstairs TV. It was quiet in the house.

Excitement rose in his voice as he continued. "It was time to do what I was there for," he said.

"I snuck up the stairway from the basement and opened the door that led to the hallway. I walked down the hallway, which is carpeted, to an area by the front door, which is not carpeted. I could see that the light was on in the living room, and saw flashing lights coming from the television."

"I sat down on the stairway and then heard Harriett's poodle barking. The dog ran from the living room to the stairway where I was sitting. I petted the dog and when Harriett called for the dog, I shooed the dog back into the living room where Harriett was.

At first I thought about just getting out of the house and not do anything. I walked to the front door and was having trouble unlocking the deadbolt on the door when the dog started barking again. I heard Harriett coming to the door from the living room and when she saw me I took the crowbar and hit her once, then twice, and possibly more than that. Harriett fell to the floor and remained there."

Arterberry said he sat back down on the stairway and closed his eyes. The dog was running back and forth from Harriett to him.

"After sitting there, playing with the dog and thinking about what I had just done, I decided I would have to do something to cover up the murder. I walked down the hallway to the kitchen and confronted Velma who was walking to the living room. She was carrying a flashlight, and as she started to walk into the living room I hit her on the head with the crowbar.

"She fell down – I don't remember hitting her more than once, but apparently I did. My mind was somewhat cloudy after the second murder, but I remember that those things did happen. My first thought was to get out of the house and I ran to the side door and opened it, then thought it would be foolish to run out where I could be seen. I didn't want the telephone to ring, so I took the phone off the hook in Velma's bedroom.

"Our original plan was to make it look like burglars committed the murders. I thought I'd better follow that plan and make it look like a burglary, so I went to the back door and unlocked it. I opened the door into the dining room and put masking tape on the outside window pane. I went out onto the back porch and pulled the door shut, then, broke the window to make it look like the house had been broken into from the outside.

"I walked back into the house and ransacked all the downstairs rooms to make it look like a burglary. I stole some jewelry and about $9 in cash. I took a pillow case off a pillow in one of the bedrooms and placed the stolen items and crowbar in the pillow case. I didn't pay much attention to the jewelry, but I recall one of the items was a rectangular-shaped watch with diamonds all around it.

"I went to the basement and turned on the hot water heater valve, allowing the water to run on the floor. I did this to wash away any footprints I might have left. I believe it was about an hour or so that I was upstairs and before I returned to the basement. After washing the basement floor I went back upstairs.

"I picked up the keys to Harriett's Mustang from the kitchen counter and entered the garage from the utility room. Before stealing Harriett's car, I removed the light bulb from the overhead door opener because I didn't want the light to come on when I left in the stolen car. I laid the light bulb in David's race car, parked next to Harriett's car. I used the garage door opener in the Mustang to open the door, and then I drove away, closing the door behind me."

Arterberry said he drove the Mustang to the rear of the Kroger store where he had parked the stolen Porsche earlier. He put the pillow case containing the stolen jewelry and the murder weapon into the Porsche and abandoned Harriett's car there.

Head spinning, emotions flying, Arterberry said he floored the stolen Porsche and drove out Central Avenue reaching speeds of 150 mph. He turned right onto King Road, slowing to an eventual stop. "I hid the pillow case and stolen jewelry in some weeds by a telephone pole and three metal markers used to mark underground gas lines," he said. Before hiding the jewelry, he took the crowbar from the pillow case.

Arterberry said he was sort of in a daze while continuing his race down secluded area roads. "I took my blood splattered shoes off and pitched them out the car window and threw the bloody gloves and crowbar in a ditch in the same area," he said.

"After disposing of the evidence, I turned the car around and returned to David and Patricia's house. It was around 9:30 p.m. when I entered the house. No one was home and I fell asleep on the couch. The telephone rang and I picked it up; it was Patricia. I can't remember if I told her that I had committed the murders, but around 11:30 p.m. they came home and I told them what happened.

"I told them about the murders and a couple of days later me and Patricia drove to King Road and picked up the pillow case with the stolen jewelry. Patricia went through the jewelry, picking out the good stuff. I drove to the Maumee/Perrysburg Bridge and threw the jewelry Patricia didn't want over the side of the bridge, into the Maumee River. I don't know what Patricia did with the stolen jewelry she kept."

15

Thanksgiving morning – Thursday, Nov. 27, 1975, around 10:15 a.m.
Second interrogation of Patricia Wernert for the murders

After David and Arterberry's interrogations, I found Patricia had not told me all the truth about the plan to kill Velma and Harriett. Nor had she told me about going with Arterberry to pick up the stolen jewelry after the murders. She also failed to say she and David went to Trilby Animal Hospital to hide the jewelry in a crawl space under the dog kennels.

I confronted her with these facts, and she admitted she had not been totally truthful when we talked earlier.

It was during this second interrogation that Patricia admitted their plan was to kill both Harriett and Velma. She said she did go with Arterberry to pick up the stolen jewelry where he hid it on King Road after the murders, and she and her husband put the stolen jewelry in a red Avon jar at Trilby Animal Hospital. She said she had a key to the hospital because she worked there, and she and David entered the hospital at night and hid the jewelry. David went into a crawl space under the dog kennels, where he buried the jar.

After clearing up the discrepancies, I confronted Patricia, David and Arterberry. They all admitted, in front of each other, that they had confessed to me about their parts in the murders. David and Patricia told Arterberry that they had given me a taped confession implicating him in the murders, and had told me he was the actual murderer of Harriett Wernert and Velma Bush.

Arterberry then asked if he could talk to the Wernerts alone. I left the room and stood outside while they talked for a few minutes. I felt this meeting could assist our investigation in two ways. It could clear up any other discrepancies I might find in the statements given by each person, and could possibly persuade Arterberry to give me a tape confession concerning the murders.

Arterberry's earlier confession was not taped, because I didn't want to take a chance he would clam up and not talk to me if he knew the conversation was being tape recorded. In most instances I first take a verbal statement, and then a tape recorded statement for this reason. If the suspect gives a verbal statement, but later refuses to give a tape recorded statement, at least I have the verbal confession.

A verbal statement is just as admissible in court as the tape recorded statement, but with the tape recorded statement the suspect can't later deny what he had told verbally.

After the meeting, David and Patricia were returned to their jail cells, and I continued my interview with Arterberry. Before returning to her cell, Patricia gave her husband a kiss on the cheek; then turned to Arterberry and gave him a long, hard kiss on the lips. One would have to wonder who the husband was and who the friend was.

Safety Building
525 North Erie Street, Toledo, Ohio
Photograph taken by Toledo Police Department photographer
Sgt. Keefe Snyder

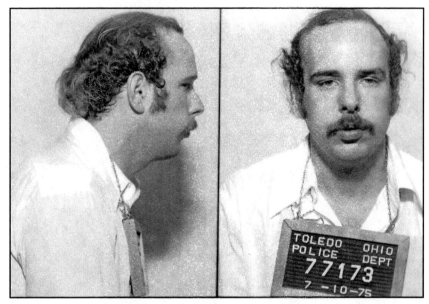

Police arrest photo of Richard Wayne Arterberry

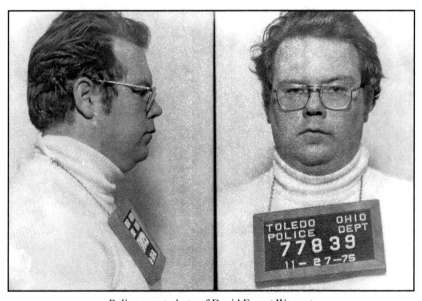

Police arrest photo of David Ernest Wernert

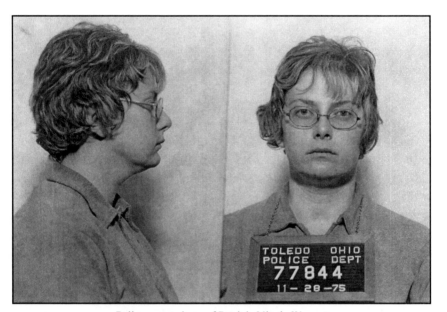

Police arrest photo of Patricia Nicole Wernert

16

Thanksgiving morning – Thursday, Nov. 27, 1975, around 10:30am
Richard Arterberry asked for an attorney

I told Arterberry, "Now that you have given a verbal statement about the murders, I would like you to go over your confession with me again, but this time I would like to tape-record your confession to show that you have been cooperative and have told me the truth."

I explained, "The taped confession is no different than your previous oral confession; it just confirms you have cooperated and have told the truth."

"I don't know about giving a taped confession," Arterberry said. "I'd better call my attorney and talk to him before I put it on tape."

As I pointed out earlier, sometimes criminals will confess verbally, but may be reluctant to put it on tape because they can't deny what they have said. If their statement isn't on tape, they might feel they can always deny they ever said what they have confessed to. Again, as far as evidentiary value goes, the verbal confession is as admissible in court as the taped confession. Investigators like to get the confessions on tape as well as verbally, because we know the criminal might later deny what he said.

A common question asked is; "Why would any criminal confess in the first place?"

Most criminals want to know what the police have on them, and what others may have said about their guilt. I have found that most will talk to you, thinking they can outsmart you. They feel they are smart enough to solicit information from you, while not incriminating themselves. Of course they are wrong; an experienced interrogator will solicit incriminating information from any guilty person who is willing to be interviewed. The information may or may not be a full disclosure, but in most cases evidence will be revealed by the perpetrator.

Once Arterberry said he wanted his attorney, I had no choice but to provide him with an attorney of his choice.

"Who is your attorney?" I asked.

"Art James, he has handled cases for me in the past," Arterberry said.

"It's Thanksgiving, he won't be at work. Do you have his home telephone number?"

"I don't remember it," Arterberry said. "He has an unlisted number."

I took Arterberry to my office where he was allowed to look through the telephone book, searching for someone who might know James' unlisted number. He was unable to locate a source for the number.

Chief Wechtel looked up the attorney's office number and called it but no one answered. It was Thanksgiving and we didn't really expect James or any of his associates to be there. I looked in the city directory but found no telephone number for the attorney, indicating he indeed did have an unlisted telephone number.

Then it dawned on me, I knew one person who might have the attorneys' telephone number; the woman Chief Wechtel and I interviewed in her basement the night before. She told us that James was Arterberry's former attorney. I called her and she furnished me with the attorneys' unlisted number.

I called attorney Arthur James.

When I reached him, I explained that Arterberry had requested to talk with him. I said Arterberry was being questioned about the murders of Velma Bush and Harriett Wernert. He agreed to represent Arterberry, and I gave him directions so he could meet with us.

"I'll be right there," James said.

James arrived at the Safety Building around 11 a.m. I advised him that Arterberry had made a full verbal confession to the murders, and that both David and Patricia Wernert had made full verbal and tape-recorded statements implicating themselves and Arterberry in the conspiracy. He entered the interviewing room and talked to Arterberry alone. After a few minutes, James came out of the room and asked me if I had promised Arterberry he would be charged with manslaughter instead of aggravated murder.

"No way," I said. "You know I can't make him any promises." Manslaughter is a lesser included offense to aggravated murder and murder, but only the prosecutors can make a decision on lesser offenses.

The attorney asked to see my Ohio Criminal Law Handbook so he could look at the aggravated murder law and lesser offenses. I provided him with the codes and he reviewed them.

I remembered what the woman told Chief Wechtel and me in the basement of her home. In a conversation she had with James she said he felt if he had not always gotten Arterberry out of trouble before, he might not have gotten involved with the Wernerts. She said James didn't know for sure whether Arterberry was involved in the murders, but felt he could be. So I knew I was dealing with a man who had a conscience, and was compassionate.

I told James that all I wanted was for him to let Arterberry make the decision whether to give me the taped confession or not. James said he would talk to him and re-entered the interviewing room.

After a few minutes, James came out and said Arterberry would give the tape statement. I asked him to sit in on the statement, but he declined. The attorney left and I took the tape-recorded confession. Arterberry repeated his earlier verbal statement, but this time the confession was tape recorded.

After taking the confessions and after all three prisoners were booked, Chief Wechtel and I went home for what remained of Thanksgiving Day. I had been without sleep for almost 60 hours, but didn't realize how exhausted I was. Chief Wechtel had been up for more than 24 hours, but was still going strong when we shook hands and told each other, "Good job."

Thanksgiving was an important holiday in our family. We always had dinner at my father Eugene's and stepmother Martha Stiles' home in Toledo's north end. My stepsisters, Janet Ocheske, Elaine Christian, and Carol Henney were there with their husbands, Roy, Danny, and Bob, and their children. Danny Christian was also a Toledo police officer, so he had an idea what Chief Wechtel and I had been through. My children, Kevin, Carey, and Amy, always looked forward to Thanksgiving with their grandparents and cousins; it was one of our favorite holidays.

During dinner my eyes fell closed at times and my mind started to shut down. We left earlier than usual that night, and when I laid my head on the pillow, I didn't move until Friday morning.

Sleep felt good, but I was up at my regular time. There was still lots of work to do, and people to talk to. Just because an arrest has been made doesn't mean an investigation is over. We still hadn't found the murder weapon or recovered the stolen jewelry. The clothing worn by Arterberry during the murders hadn't been located and we still had to investigate other crimes Arterberry told us about.

I showered, shaved, and kissed the sleeping family goodbye. I was ready for another day.

17
In The Mind Of A Killer

What is in the mind of a killer?

What compels one human being to murder another?

Is it environment, genes, or merely the excitement of killing and watching someone die?

What does a killer look like?

Can we identify a killer from the average person, or could our neighbor, fellow employee, or friend be a monster instead of the pleasant person he seems to be?

What made Patricia Wernert encourage her husband David to murder his mother and grandmother?

How could David Wernert betray the trust of his mother and grandmother by plotting their murders?

Why did Richard Arterberry conspire to bludgeon Harriett Wernert and Velma Bush to death?

What possibly could have led the three of them to agree that the women should be killed so mercilessly and painfully?

One never knows what lurks in the mind of a killer!

After spending twelve hours interrogating the three murderers, I tried to understand how they could cold-bloodily plan and carry out the murders of two innocent women. Not only were they defenseless women, they were David Wernert's mother and grandmother.

During Richard Arterberry's confession he gave the appearance that he actually enjoyed the experience of killing Harriett and Velma. David Wernert probably described it best when he told me he thought Arterberry killed his mother and grandmother for a new experience and the excitement of taking someone's life. Wernert said Arterberry had been involved in many things in his young life and he felt this was a just another challenge for him.

When confessing, Arterberry described the murders with no sign of remorse. He talked about the killings, showing no respect for life. When I asked him why he murdered the women he said the Wernerts told him the women were sickly and gave him the impression he would actually be doing them a favor. Patricia Wernert lied to him and told him she had cancer and wanted the women's inheritance so she could enjoy the short time she had left. He was not offered any specific amount of money to commit the murders but felt he would be taken care of after the Wernerts got the inheritance. "I really don't know why I did it," he said.

Arterberry was like most of the other murderers I have taken confessions from. In his own sick way he tried to excuse the horrible thing he did by thinking I would believe this was a mercy killing. I sided with what David told me: Arterberry murdered the women for the thrill of it, not for money, although he expected to be taken care of after David received the inheritance.

When Arterberry and I concluded his tape-recorded confession, I asked him if there was anything else he wanted to say and he said he could probably rattle on for hours but in fact had told me all that had happened. Arterberry wasn't sorry for what he did and actually enjoyed talking about it.

Some people kill for money, revenge, or hatred of another and some kill for the pure excitement and rush it gives them. My assessment of Arterberry led me to believe he murdered for the rush; and excitement; money was an attraction but not the driving force.

Patricia Wernert's confession led me to believe she was the instigator behind the killings. It was her greed for the inheritance and hatred of her mother-in-law, Harriett Wernert, that compelled her to coax her husband and Arterberry into murdering the women. She gave the appearance that ice water ran through her veins, and love and remorse didn't appear in her vocabulary. Her personality was exposed by the witchcraft she practiced and the evil of her ways. Her manipulative influence encouraged her husband and Arterberry to carry out her unthinkable plan.

When confessing, Arterberry told me Patricia talked about killing David after Harriett and Velma were taken care of. She had no love for David; she married him for his money, Arterberry and others we interviewed said. She wanted the inheritance for herself, so David would be next.

One might be convinced that Arterberry and Patricia Wernert's background could have led them to murder. Even though there was some evidence that Arterberry had a very high IQ, neither he nor Patricia went any further than high school, and both carried average grades. Both came from broken homes, used drugs, showed no respect for life or people, and wanted more than their abilities would produce.

David Wernert had certain positives that make it all the more inexplicable as to why he would become a murderer of his mother and grandmother. He came from wealthy parents, received a higher level of education, graduating from Ottawa Hills High School, the second best high school in the state, and receiving a bachelors' degree in business.

While attending the University of Toledo, he was in the ROTC program, and shortly after graduating he married Patricia and joined the Army. He was commissioned a 2nd lieutenant, serving over 9 years and rising to the rank of captain. He was an Ordnance Ammo Officer and served a tour of duty in Vietnam. His duties included conducting search and destroy missions. He received the National

Defense Service Medal, Vietnam Service Medal, Vietnam Campaign Medal, and was honorably discharged in August of 1969.

After David's discharge from the Army, he worked for his father for awhile and after his father died he became the parts department manager for Will Dennis Volkswagen. He moved into his grandmother's home on Christie Street in Toledo.

David didn't have to murder his mother and grandmother for the inheritance: They gave him money when he needed it, and he lived in his grandmother's house for free. She had moved from the home into the Emkay house with her daughter, David's mother Harriett. He and his brother, James Scott Wernert, were to inherit their mother and grandmothers estate upon their death, so why would David want to murder them?

David told me that he took part in the murders because his mother and grandmother were getting old and complained of being ill and in pain all the time. He said they became more of a burden to him, and his brother was of no help because he lived in California. I agreed with what Arterberry told me, that this was a sick rationalization of the whole thing.

Perhaps the reason for David's participation was a combination of things. He was tired of taking care of his mother and grandmother, and life would be easier when he inherited their estate and had control of all the money. He was coaxed by his wife into eliminating the women and his combat stint in Vietnam, conducting search and destroy missions, may have hardened him against the love he once had for Harriett and Velma.

Assuredly, most people would agree that none of the killers' reasons for committing the murders make sense. But when dealing with the twisted and sick minds of sociopaths, not much does.

18

One Crime Leads To Another

Oct. 20, 1975
Stolen radio and 8-track tape player

While I was interrogating Arterberry about the stolen Porsche, he admitted he had installed a stolen Courier citizen band radio and a Realistic 8-track tape player in the car.

During that interview, Arterberry said he bought the radio, along with the tape player, for $50 from a man at Walt's Den Tavern.

"I was working as a bartender there when the guy sold them to me," he said. He didn't know his name, but was told the radio and tape player were hot.

The stolen Porsche was released to Will Dennis Volkswagen before we had a chance to remove the stolen CB radio and 8 track tape player.

I recovered the items on Tuesday, Dec. 2, from Robert Vergiels, the office manager at the dealership. I checked theft reports at the

Toledo police records section, and found that the CB had been stolen from the car of Harold Reid of Perrysburg, Ohio.

The radio was stolen from his car while it was parked on St. Clair Street in Toledo on Oct. 20, 1975. I was unable to locate a theft report for the stolen tape player. The radio was later returned to Mr. Reid and the tape player was placed in the Toledo police property room until an owner could be found.

Sept. 20, 1975
Stolen car from Glass City Dodge

During Arterberry's interrogation, he told me about stealing a 1969 green Plymouth Roadrunner from Glass City Dodge on West Alexis Road. He said his friend, Ronald Wyatt, had blown the motor in his '69 Plymouth and needed a working engine.

Arterberry told me it was him, Patricia Wernert, and Wyatt who stole the car, and he surmised that Patricia put him up to it to see if he had the nerve to steal it. After looking back at the whole scenario, he felt Patricia was testing him to see if he had enough nerve to murder Velma Bush and Harriett Wernert.

"I hotwired and stole the car while Patricia and Wyatt acted as lookouts. The engine from the stolen car was later put into Wyatt's car," he said. He junked the chassis at Kasle Iron and Metal Company on Lagrange Street.

Dec. 2, 1975, 10:45 a.m.
Interrogation of Ronald Wyatt for stolen car

Chief Wechtel and I questioned Wyatt in my office. He gave a verbal and taped confession admitting his part in the theft of the car.

"I knew they would tell on me, I just knew it. I never did anything like this before. Arterberry made it sound so easy and was so convincing that we would never get caught, but here I am," Wyatt said.

"I was staying with Patricia and David Wernert at the time we stole the Roadrunner. I had been staying with the Wernerts on and off since the middle of September. Richard Arterberry was also staying with them. I mentioned to Patricia and Arterberry that I blew the engine in my Roadrunner.

"'You need an engine? I can get you an engine,' Arterberry told him. 'Hotwiring a Plymouth is like taking candy from a baby.'"

"On Saturday, Sept. 20, we drove around searching for a car to steal. I was riding with Patricia in her Triumph and Arterberry followed us in a red Ford van he borrowed from another friend of ours, Craig Bedra."

Wyatt said they drove by Glass City Dodge and saw that they had a green 1969 Plymouth Roadrunner like his. They drove back to the Wernerts' house and decided to steal it. They left for Glass City Dodge in Patricia's Mercury. He said she parked in a car wash next to the dealership. Wyatt and Patricia acted as lookouts while Arterberry hotwired the Roadrunner.

Arterberry drove the stolen car to Bedra's garage on Prouty Street while Patricia and Wyatt followed in the Mercury. The car was stored in Bedra's garage for two or three weeks until they had a chance to transfer the engine to Wyatt's car. He said Bedra didn't know the car was stolen.

Wyatt said he and Arterberry took the stolen Roadrunner to A & A Salvage Company in Toledo's south end. "Arterberry used to have a business interest in this salvage and auto repair company," he said.

David Wernert drove up, and a man who worked for A & A Salvage helped them take the engine from the stolen car with a tow truck hoist. The man did not know the Roadrunner was stolen. They took both the engine and transmission and left the car at the salvage company overnight.

"The next day, Arterberry and I used Craig Bedra's van to haul the stolen engine and transmission to Bedra's garage. Bedra never knew the car parts were stolen, nor did he know they had stolen the Plymouth they were removed from," Wyatt said.

"At the time, I was working for Tambers Construction Company, and I used their van to transport the stolen Roadrunner engine from Bedra's garage to Bails Garage on Superior Street," Wyatt said. The owners, Bob and Harry Bails, came to Bedra's garage and used a tow truck to put the stolen engine into the van so it could be transported to their shop. He said the stolen engine was put into his Plymouth Roadrunner at Bails' garage, and he paid them for hooking the engine up. Wyatt said Bob and Harry Bails never knew the engine was taken from the stolen car.

"Where is your car with the stolen engine now?" I asked.

"It's parked in front of the police station – I drove it here this morning," he said.

I had already verified the car was stolen by checking stolen car reports, and by talking to the used car manager at Glass City Dodge, Roy Taulbee. I had Wyatt's car, with the stolen engine, towed to Sobbs Towing Service, and I arrested Wyatt for grand theft auto. Wyatt was booked in the city jail and Chief Wechtel and I continued our investigation.

We questioned Bedra about the stolen car and he verified he let Arterberry and Wyatt keep it in his garage, but he didn't know the car was stolen.

Chief Wechtel and I questioned Harold Reddick, owner of A & A Salvage and Ray's Wrecking Company. He admitted he helped Arterberry and Wyatt take the engine and transmission out.

"I never knew the car was stolen," Reddick said. "Arterberry gave me the green Plymouth Roadrunner for helping them pull the engine and transmission from the car," he continued.

Monday Sept. 22, 1975, 11:55 p.m.
Aggravated Robbery of the
Holland Tavern in Holland, Ohio

After Chief Wechtel and I arrested Arterberry, his personal property was confiscated. During the inventory, we found he had a Sohio credit card in the name of Alice Y. Collins. The card was signed William F. Collins with an expiration date of 04/76.

During my interview with Arterberry, I asked where he got the card.

"From my friend, Larry Masters," he said. "Larry and another friend of ours, Charles Caldwell Jr., told me they robbed the Holland Tavern with a sawed-off shotgun, and that the credit card was among the things they stole from the patrons. While I was working as a bartender at Walt's Den Tavern in September, the police came into the bar looking for someone. Larry was afraid they were going to arrest him, so he slipped me the stolen card, and I've had it ever since."

Arterberry said he was staying with Caldwell and Masters at the time. "They were living in an apartment on Lorain Street in south Toledo," he said. "I didn't know it at the time, but after loaning them my `69 Chevy Nova, I found out they used the car to commit the robbery."

Masters and Caldwell told him the shotgun they used belonged to Charles Caldwell Sr., who is a Toledo police officer, and who also operates the Whistle Stop Bar on Broadway. Arterberry said Mr. Caldwell did not know his son used the gun, nor did he know anything about the robbery.

After my interview with Arterberry, we contacted Holland Chief of Police, Frank Reitmeier. He verified that two white men wearing dark colored nylon stockings and armed with a shotgun robbed the bartender and several patrons in the late evening of Sept. 22. They fled in one of the patrons' cars but abandoned it nearby.

In addition, Chief Reitmeier discovered that the same two robbers, wearing the same mask and armed with the same shotgun, had robbed Spy's Inn on August 28. The owner of the bar, Olie Spy, was robbed of cash and his car. The car was located not far from the bar.

We told Chief Reitmeier about our arrest of Arterberry for the murders, and about recovering the stolen credit card from Arterberry at the time of his arrest. We provided the chief with the card and with Arterberry's statement implicating Masters and Caldwell.

Chief Reitmeier was informed that we had checked the police

records of Masters and Caldwell and found that both men had previous criminal records. We furnished the chief with their records and personal statistics.

Through the information and evidence we turned over, Chief Reitmeier, with the assistance of the Lucas County Sheriff's Department, was able to build a strong case and arrest and convict both men for the Holland Tavern robbery. As a result of a plea agreement, both men admitted robbing both bars.

Caldwell's father was one of my first partners on the Toledo police force. He, Bill Rowen, and I were assigned to the downtown Toledo scout car. We worked together for almost two years and Charlie, as he preferred we call him, taught me many important things about police work. He was the senior officer on the unit and I respected his honesty, integrity, courage, and knowledge of police work. He was a great street cop and had extraordinary instincts. He could spot trouble before it happened and could quiet and extinguish a potentially explosive situation before it got out of hand.

Charlie worked hard to get ahead, taking off-duty jobs to support and raise his children. His 17-year-old sister, Mary Caldwell, was murdered several years before. She and her boyfriend, Edward Lee Mitchell, of Liberty Center, Ohio, were killed and burned in the boyfriend's car while parked in a lover's lane near Centennial and Angola roads in western Lucas County. Charlie spent a lot of time investigating the murders himself, but no arrest was ever made. Toledo police detective Robert Baumgartner developed suspects, but there was insufficient evidence to make an arrest.

The arrest of Charlie's son was very difficult for him, and he blamed his working hours away from home as possibly contributing to the problems. Charlie died several years later.

19
Strengthening The Charges

Even when an arrest has been made, experienced detectives know the investigation is never over until every lead is followed and all possible evidence collected. I prepare every case with the attitude that the case is going to trial. It would be a mistake for an investigator to feel the case is complete, just because an arrest was made.

I contacted Toledo police artist, James Carnes, to do a sketch of the Ottawa Hills murder scene. Detective Carnes was not only an excellent artist, but an experienced investigator as well. He understood the need for an accurate sketch of the murder scene, including the locations of the victims and evidence.

Carnes drew to scale the first floor and basement areas of the home at 2130 Emkay. Carnes' sketch included a detailed drawing of where the victims were located, the position of the bodies when found, and the location of the evidence. The sketch helps the judge and jury visualize what occurred, where it occurred, and how the murders took place. Photographs also assist in doing this, but they only capture one area at a time. The sketches provide a collective picture of the crime scene.

Friday, Nov. 28, 1975, 12:05 p.m.
Recovery of jewelry stolen from murder scene

During my interrogations of David and Patricia Wernert, they told me that after Arterberry gave Patricia the stolen jewelry, they hid it in a crawl space under the dog kennels at her place of employment, Trilby Animal Hospital. David even drew me a map of where he hid the jewelry and described how he dropped down through the trapdoor in the utility closet, to the crawl space under the kennels. He had crawled under the kennels and buried the jewelry in an Avon jar.

I called the Trilby Animal Hospital on Friday, Nov. 28, and talked to employee Sandra Bails. She said Dr. Burns and his family were visiting relatives for the Thanksgiving holiday, and she gave me the telephone number where he could be reached. I immediately called and explained about the hidden jewelry. He gave me permission to go to the animal hospital and retrieve it.

At the hospital Chief Wechtel and I were directed to a utility closet where the trapdoor was located. The utility closet housed the hot water heater, electric circuit breaker box, and water pipes. A top the trapdoor was a plastic container.

Following the map Wernert had drawn, I dropped into the crawl space. I crawled through the dirt along the block foundation wall to an opening leading to another area under the kennels. I dug beneath the dirt, about three or four inches, and located the Avon jar containing the jewelry.

We found a woman's 14-karat white gold Bulova wristwatch, a woman's 14-karat yellow gold Elgin pendant watch and chain, a 14-karat white gold diamond watchband with 28 diamonds located on the sides of the watchband, a 14-karat white gold Harvill diamond wristwatch, a 14-karat yellow gold pearl ring with five pearls across the front, a two-strand pearl necklace, and a pearl necklace strand.

I called for a crime scene technician to come to the hospital and take photographs. Larry Mallory arrived and took photos of the crawl space and the evidence.

On Sunday, Nov. 30, Chief Wechtel took the jewelry to Keidan's Jewelers to have it appraised. The owner, Sherman Goldstein, estimated it at $1,585.

Friday, Nov. 28, 1975
Freda Sorby

Once arrests have been made, it sometimes inspires witnesses to come forward with information. Such was the case with Freda Sorby, age 69. Ms. Sorby contacted the Ottawa Hills police dispatcher and said she might have some information about the murders.

Ms. Sorby was in Mercy Hospital after having minor surgery when she called police. Officers Paul Hanslik and William Snell went there to interview her.

"I have no direct information about the murders, other than what I have read in the newspaper," she said. She had been friends of Harriett Wernert and Velma Bush for many years, and had visited and called frequently.

"The last time I talked to Velma Bush on the telephone was Monday evening, Nov. 17. Velma said her grandson, David Wernert, pushed her onto her bed while demanding money. Velma said David had a habit of taking money from her purse without her consent, and at times he treated her like dirt."

That information gave us insight into Wernert's attitude and treatment of his grandmother. If he treated her this way, there was reason to believe he treated his mother that way as well. Ms. Sorby's conversation with the officers also indicated that Wernert's greed for money suggests that he might resort to violence to get it.

Jeri and Chuck Machala

Jeri and Chuck Machala came forward and told me that they were good friends with Harriett Wernert and Velma Bush. They met the women at church and visited them on occasion.

Jeri said she and her husband would stop over after eating out at the Yankee Doodle restaurant on Sylvania Avenue. She said Harriett and Velma enjoyed company, so they would stop by around 6:30 p.m. after eating. "Harriett loved Manhattan cocktails and they sipped a few while talking," she said.

Chuck collected old porcelain dolls and Harriett had a doll head she promised to give him one day.

The Machalas said they knew Harriett's son and saw him at the Ottawa Hills home a few days before the women were murdered. David wanted $5,000 claiming his wife had to have surgery to remove a growth on her leg. The Machalas said they were suspicious that the demand for money might be a lie when Harriett said she would have to visit Patricia in the hospital and David replied that she could not have visitors.

When I asked if Harriett or Velma ever mentioned that David and Patricia were mean to them, the Machalas said no. "We knew of no problems like that," they said.

"We were shocked at Harriett and Velma's deaths and the arrests. To think we were there around the time they were murdered is scary," Jeri said.

Nov. 28, 1975
Additional interview with Richard Arterberry

Arterberry's attorney, Arthur James, gave consent for his client to be further interviewed. The main purpose for the additional interview was to take Arterberry for a ride and so he could point out where he threw the murder weapon; the gloves he wore during the murders; his bloody shoes; and the place he hid the stolen jewelry.

Arterberry agreed to go on the ride and show us where he had discarded the evidence.

Retracing the trail Arterberry took when fleeing the murder scene was like being in the mind of the killer.

Arterberry told how he fled in Harriett Wernert's Mustang, racing to the Kroger parking lot behind the Westgate Shopping Center.

There he changed cars, now driving the stolen Porsche he and David Wernert had hidden behind the store so he could change cars after the murders, making it harder to pursue and detect his escape route.

Once we examined the escape route from the murder scene to the Kroger store, Arterberry continued tracing his movements.

"I drove behind the stores in the shopping center and headed toward Secor Road. As I passed behind Lanes Drug Store, I threw a roll of tape out the window into the parking lot. This was the same roll of tape I used to tape the old ladies back door window with before breaking the glass to make it look like a burglary had occurred," he said.

We looked for the roll of tape, but it was nowhere to be found.

Continuing on, Arterberry directed Chief Wechtel to drive west on Central Avenue, and I could see a difference in the look on Arterberry's face. It was as if he was again experiencing the excitement of that night. His adrenalin was pumping as he explained the thrill of driving the Porsche in excess of 100 mph. "Can you believe I had that Porsche traveling 150 mph? Not a cop around – at that speed they couldn't have caught me if they tried."

As we were approaching King Road, he told Chief Wechtel to slow down. He said he threw the leather gloves and the latex gloves he wore during the killings in this area. "It's hard to say for sure exactly where I threw them – I was going so fast, it's hard to say," Arterberry said.

I searched the area, but because of the roadside underbrush and earlier fallen snow, I had no luck. The snowplows had made the search more difficult because they had piled snow along the sides of the road. I documented all the areas Arterberry pointed out so we could send police officers back to the area for more thorough searches. When the snow melted, the search would be made much easier.

We continued driving west on Central Avenue when Arterberry said, "Turn right onto King Road. I hid the pillow case containing the stolen jewelry in the weeds by those metal markers." He pointed out three markers used to identify underground wires and pipelines.

Near the markers was a telephone pole. I copied the number

from the telephone pole so we could identify the area where the jewelry had been hidden. Of course, we knew the jewelry had already been moved by Arterberry and Patricia Wernert, because we had recovered it from the Trilby Animal Hospital.

Our next direction was west on Central. When we approached Kilburn Road, Arterberry told Chief Wechtel to turn right. He pointed out an area where he threw the crowbar he used to bludgeon the women with.

He pointed to a ditch on the west side of the road and said, "I believe this is where I got rid of the crowbar." I searched the area, but was unable to locate it. Again, because of the heavy underbrush and snow, I found it impossible to complete a thorough search.

"Do you want me to show you where I threw my earth shoes? I threw them away because I was afraid you could match footprints I left in the house," he said.

"Where do you want me to go?" Chief Wechtel asked.

He directed Wechtel to drive down Sylvania Avenue between Holland-Sylvania Road and Corey Road, near the bridge that crosses the creek.

Arterberry pointed to an area west of the road and said, "I believe that is where I threw them, but I may be mistaken." I searched the area but again I found nothing.

"Is there anyplace else you want to show us?" I asked.

"Just one more place," Arterberry said.

He directed us to Conant Street in Maumee, then midway across the Maumee/Perrysburg Bridge. "Stop here," he instructed.

He told us that a few days after he hid the pillow case with the stolen jewelry, he and Patricia Wernert retrieved it. Patricia went through the case picking out the pieces she knew to be of value. After she sorted out what was real and what was costume jewelry, he threw the costume jewelry over the bridge into the Maumee River. "Patricia kept the good stuff," Arterberry said. He said he did not know what she did with the jewelry she kept.

We drove to the Ottawa Hills station where Chief Wechtel got the jewelry from his safe. This was the same jewelry he and

I recovered from the animal hospital. We showed Arterberry the recovered stolen jewelry and he looked at it.

Arterberry identified all of the items with the exception of the pearl ring as being part of the jewelry he stole from the Emkay house. He said the ring could also be one of the pieces he stole, but he doesn't remember it.

I felt the trip had been successful, and I was surprised at Arterberry's cooperation and attitude. He seemed to have enjoyed the trip and gave every impression that he liked telling us about the murders and his escape.

Arterberry was taken back to jail – his new home of solitude.

Monday, Dec. 1, 1975
Further questioning of Richard Arterberry about the clothing he wore and the murder weapons he used during the murders.

Chief Wechtel and I again questioned Arterberry, this time at the jail. We were still trying to locate and identify one of the murder weapons used during the murders, and also the clothing he wore during the murders.

I didn't feel Arterberry was lying to us; in fact, he seemed to be fully cooperative. When someone commits an act as heinous as these murders, they sometimes get confused or try to put certain elements of the crime out of their mind. We were just trying to jog Arterberry's memory and strengthen our case even more. As long as the killer was willing to talk, we were willing to listen.

"Richard, I know we have discussed these things earlier, but it is important that we can show that you are cooperating and being truthful. Are you sure of the area you threw the crowbar?"

Arterberry said that to the best of his recollection, he pointed out the area he threw the crowbar. "I was driving very fast when I threw it out of the window, and the crowbar may be further down the road," he said.

"How about the clothing you wore?"

"I was wearing blue jeans, a Levi jacket, and my brown earth shoes," he said. He couldn't remember what shirt he had on.

"What did you do with the clothing?" I asked.

"I believe the jeans are the ones I was arrested in and the shirt and Levi jacket would still be at the Wernerts' home," he said. He added that he didn't see any blood on his clothing, but realized there must have been some. He said Patricia Wernert washed all his clothing after the murders.

I had confiscated Arterberry's clothing after his arrested so I had the jeans he was talking about. At that same time I also confiscated his red and white short-sleeve shirt, and a pair of black wool socks he was wearing. The clothing was tested and Laboratory results proved negative for traces of blood. Arterberry was either mistaken about the clothing he wore during the murders, or the washing of the clothing destroyed all traces of the blood.

I informed Arterberry that a hammer was found in the basement of the Emkay house. I located it on the workbench, and when tested for blood by our crime lab, traces of blood were found. "Did you use the hammer as one of the weapons?" I asked.

Arterberry said no. "I do remember laying the crowbar on the workbench, next to the hammer, after I did the killings, and possibly blood from the crowbar got onto the hammer before I took the crowbar with me."

I said, "Look, Richard, the coroner said that in addition to the crowbar, a hammer was also used to strike Harriett. Is it possible that after you bludgeoned the ladies with the crowbar, you took the hammer from the basement workbench and struck Harriett with the hammer, perhaps to make sure she was dead and to make it look like more than one person did the killings?" He looked at me inquisitively, and said, "I may have, but I don't remember doing that."

During this same interview I asked that Arterberry give us permission to search his apartment on Summit Street. I told him we wanted to search the apartment for any clothing he might have worn, property that may have been taken from the murder scene, and any other evidence that may be connected to the murders. He agreed to the search and signed a waiver to that affect.

I also questioned him about the two safe deposit box keys I found on the key ring I took from him at the time of his arrest. This is the same key ring that held the key to the stolen Porsche.

"Where do those keys belong, and what is in those boxes?" I asked.

Arterberry said the boxes were rented at First Federal Savings and Loan in West Toledo. He said he didn't recall what if anything was in the boxes. I advised him that we had confiscated an exact key for one of his boxes from Patricia Wernert, at the time of her arrest. Why did she have a duplicate key to the box?

He said he didn't know why she had it, but she must have stolen it from him. "She asked me if she could have her name put on the box so she could use it, but I never added her name to the box," he said. When I questioned Particia Wernert about the key, during my interrogations of her, she denied any knowledge of the key or how it got on her key ring.

Arterberry signed another waiver, but this time it was for us to search the deposit boxes.

Monday, Dec. 1, 1975, 7:10 p.m.
Execution of the search warrant waiver for
Richard Arterberry's apartment at 2039 Summit St.

I called Walter Staerker, owner of the apartment at 2039 Summit, and advised him that Chief Wechtel and I wanted to search the apartment of Richard Arterberry. I told him Arterberry had signed a waiver of search, and he agreed to meet us there with a key.

Staerker said he had known Arterberry for a long time and that Arterberry worked part-time as a bartender for him at his place, Walt's Den on South Street. He said he pretty much allowed Arterberry to live in the apartment for free.

"I have something I want to give you," Mr. Staerker said. He handed me a black wallet and said Arterberry left it in a drawer at the bar. He said his barmaid, Sandra Harmon, gave the wallet to him after Arterberry was arrested.

I inventoried the wallet immediately. It contained no money, just personal papers. Inside was Arterberry's draft card and Social Security card, a business card for attorney John Weglian, an attorney in the same law office as Arterberry's attorney, Arthur James, and assorted personal papers.

After searching Arterberry's apartment, the only thing confiscated was a cash receipt from Will Dennis Porsche/Audi Inc., dated Nov. 13, 1975, and made out to Arterberry for $40. The receipt indicated the money was for a deposit on a 1974 Porsche and the salesman was D. Gorin. This was the receipt Arterberry told me he received when putting a deposit on the Porsche he later stole. The receipt corroborated his confession to me.

Monday, Dec. 1, 1975
Execution of second search warrant
for the home of David and Patricia Wernert.

After questioning Arterberry at the county jail, I decided to seek another search warrant for the home of Patricia and David Wernert.

I wanted to search the house for the denim jacket and any other clothes Arterberry wore during the murders.

After the warrant was authorized, I contacted Harriett Wernert and Velma Bush's estate attorney, Edward Hoffman, and he assisted Chief Wechtel and me in executing the warrant. Hoffman had a key to the house and was in control of the property.

Along with other clothing, I confiscated two denim jackets. One was dark blue, and the other was light blue. Both jackets were found in the same downstairs closet.

While talking to Hoffman during the search he advised me that he had Patricia Wernert's key to the Trilby Animal Hospital where she was employed. He said Patricia's attorney, Peter Wagner, gave the key to him and said he obtained it from her personal property at the city jail. The key had been taken when she was booked.

Hoffman turned the key over to me and I later compared it with her employer's key. The two keys matched.

I also submitted the jackets and other clothing seized with the search warrant to the Lab for analysis. No blood was found.

Tuesday, Dec. 2, 1975, 1:30 p.m.
Execution of the search warrant waiver
for Richard Arterberry's safe deposit boxes.

On Dec. 2, Chief Wechtel and I went to First Federal Savings and Loan. With the assistance of the bank manager, Russell Comers, we executed the warrant for Richard Arterberry's safe deposit boxes.

One box contained 18 dollar bills, 8 rolls of dimes, and 3 rolls of quarters.

The other box contained 19 dollar bills, 5 rolls of dimes, 2 rolls of quarters, and 1 roll of halves.

Arterberry last opened the boxes on Nov. 18.

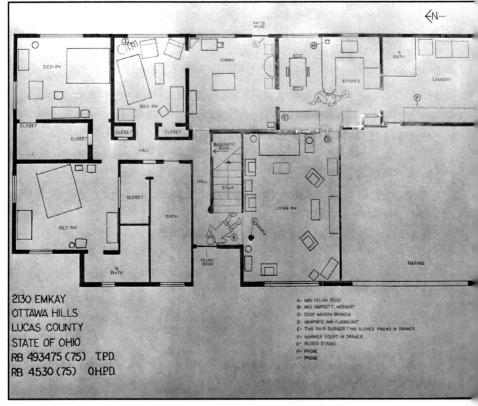

Sketch of murder scene at 2130 Emkay Drive
Drawn by Toledo Police Artist
Det. James Carnes

Trilby Animal Hospital
2736 Tremainsville Road, Toledo, Ohio

Trapdoor leading from utility room
to crawl space under dog kennels

Crawl space where victim's stolen
jewelry was buried

Recovered Avon jar with victim's stolen jewelry

20
Grand Jury Indictments

The Grand Jury hearing for Arterberry and the Wernerts was held on Dec. 4, 1975, in the Lucas County Common Pleas Courthouse.

Grand Jury proceedings are closed to the public and the evidence presented by law enforcement and witnesses is confidential. Law enforcement present testimony to nine citizens selected to perform the duty of grand jurors. Sometimes defendants may ask to testify in their own behalf at the Grand Jury hearing. Depending on the circumstances of the case, the request may or may not be granted. In this particular case the defendants did not testify, nor did they request to.

The prosecutor presenting the crimes instructs the jurors on the law pertaining to the charges under consideration. The jurors do not decide the guilt or innocence of a defendant. Their responsibility is to determine if sufficient evidence exists to require the accused to stand trial.

When the proceedings began, Lucas County assistant prosecutor James D. Bates introduced each witness to the jurors.

Sgt. David Anmahian and Officer John Nyitray were asked to tell how they were dispatched to the scene of the murders, and to their discovery of the bludgeoned bodies of Velma Bush and her daughter, Harriett Wernert.

Ottawa Hills Chief Edward Wechtel was called to testify about the circumstances of the murders, managing his officers on the case, and his work as my partner during the investigation and arrests.

I was called to describe the interrogations and confessions from the defendants, and the arrests of the three accused murderers.

When I finished testifying, a woman juror looked me in the eye and with a soft voice said, "Thank you, Detective Stiles, for your dedication and hard work." I felt a sense of pride for Chief Wechtel, the officers who assisted in the investigation, and for me. It is not the money, recognition, or security of the job that keeps good officers struggling to be successful; it is the pride of working hard and succeeding in bringing the criminals to justice. And sometimes it is the simple thank you from the citizens we serve.

Here is what the Grand Jury found and reported:

"We the Jurors of the Grand Jury of the State of Ohio, within and for Lucas County, on our oaths, in the name and by the authority of the State of Ohio, do find and present that Richard Wayne Arterberry, Patricia Nicole Wernert, and David Ernest Wernert, on or about the 18th day of November, 1975, in Lucas County, Ohio, did purposely, and with prior calculation and design, cause the deaths of Velma Bush and Harriett Wernert, in violation of 2903.01 (A) of the Ohio Revised Code, contrary to the form of the statute in such case made and provided, and against the peace and dignity of the State of Ohio."

The jurors found that the offenses were committed for hire while committing aggravated burglary and the course of conduct involved the purposeful killing of two or more persons.

If convicted, all three of the defendants could be sentenced to two separate death penalties, one for Velma Bush and one for Harriett Wernert.

21
Investigation Continues

Chief Wechtel and I were pleased with the grand jury indictments because they held those responsible for the horrible deaths of Harriett Wernert and Velma Bush accountable. Arterberry and the Wernerts were now facing what they had bestowed upon their victims – death.

We had a strong case, but no case can be invincible. We still hadn't found one of the murder weapons or the bloody clothing, gloves, and shoes Arterberry wore during the murders. I also wanted to interview Arterberry's friends, Charles Caldwell Jr. and Larry Masters, whom he ran with, and lived with, at times.

We knew Caldwell and Masters were close friends because they had used Arterberry's car to rob the Holland Tavern and Masters had given him a credit card stolen from one of the patrons they robbed. Chief Wechtel and I weren't interested in the robbery investigation, because we had turned that over to Holland. I knew both robbers were in the Lucas County Jail for the bar robbery, so they wouldn't be hard to find.

At the time of the bar robbery, Arterberry was staying with Caldwell and Masters. I felt that with this connection Arterberry may have told the robbers about murdering Velma and Harriett. If Arterberry told them about the murders, they could be good witnesses.

Chief Wechtel had a meeting with several of his officers and told them of the locations Arterberry had pointed out to us – locations where he said he threw the murder weapon, clothing, gloves and brown earth shoes he wore during the murders. The heavy snow on the ground had melted some, so this search would be easier.

On Sunday Dec. 7, Ottawa Hills Police Sgt. David Janowiecki and officers Paul Hanslik, William Snell and Christian Lopinski began their search. They searched along King Road where he had thrown the latex and leather gloves he wore; Kilburn Road, where Arterberry said he threw the crowbar he used, and Sylvania Avenue, where he said he threw his brown earth shoes after the murders.

The officers searched diligently, but the only thing they found was one of the brown earth shoes. They found it in the area Arterberry had pointed out to Chief Wechtel and me. The shoe was located about a foot from the road, down an incline, in the underbrush.

The crowbar, the other shoe, the bloody gloves, and the clothing were never found.

Dec. 29, 1975, 2:30 p.m.
Interview with Larry Masters

Chief Wechtel and I interviewed Arterberry's friend, Larry Masters, at the Lucas County Jail, where he was awaiting trial for the robbery of the Holland Tavern. He had been held in the Kalamazoo, Michigan jail for carrying a concealed weapon when served with the warrant for the Holland Tavern robbery.

Masters was a cocky guy and had the kind of face that spelled arrogance and distrust. He was a tough Toledo south-ender with a heavy drinking problem. Looking much older than his 21 years, Masters had been on the wrong side of the law for most of his life.

"What do you guys want?" Masters asked.

"A little of your time – unless you have something more important to do," I replied. My remark brought a slight smile to his hardened face.

I told Masters we wanted to talk about Arterberry. I said, "You guys were pretty close friends, I understand."

Masters said they were, and admitted they had been arrested together for carrying concealed weapons in the past. "We hung out and drank together once in awhile," he said.

"You know, your buddy has been arrested for the aggravated murders of two elderly women in Ottawa Hills."

"Yeah, I heard that."

"Since you guys were buddies, we feel he may have told you about the murders or maybe even asked you to help him kill the old ladies," I continued.

"No, he never mentioned anything to me about murdering anyone. I was arrested for the concealed weapon charge in Kalamazoo on Nov. 29 and I didn't hear about the murders until after I was arrested. I really don't know much about the murders, except what I read in the papers and heard."

Were my suspicions wrong? Maybe or maybe not, but it was obvious Masters wasn't going to admit anything, even if Arterberry told him about the murders. Perhaps he felt he was in enough trouble and didn't want to take a chance of getting in deeper. Then again maybe Arterberry never told him about the murders.

"Thanks, Larry," I said, as Wechtel and I watched the deputy take Masters back to his cell. We knew if Masters was convicted for the aggravated robbery of the tavern, he would have a lot of time to think about his life, and time to dry out from his drinking problem. People like Masters become adaptive to being institutionalized - even on the outside, they somewhat live in captivity.

I had a strong feeling prison wouldn't teach Larry Masters any lessons. My suspicions proved correct - after Masters was paroled for the Holland Tavern robbery, he went back to his old ways.

Masters hooked up with career criminal Cletus Betts. Betts had an extensive felony record and a serious drug problem. Betts shared his plan to rob a Roman Catholic priest who he knew was to make a church bank deposit at First National Bank in Toledo. Masters agreed to be the look-out while Betts snatched the bank deposit from the priest.

It was May 3, 1982, when Cletus Betts approached Father Gerald Robinson as he walked to the bank with the deposit. Father Robinson carried almost $7,000 in a leather carrying case and didn't notice Betts racing up from behind. Betts grabbed the case and fled with the money while Masters stood nearby as the look-out.

Masters caught up with Betts but could not keep pace as two witnesses to the robbery took chase. The witnesses apprehended Masters, but Betts escaped.

Masters rolled over on Betts, telling police where to find him. Betts was arrested and both pled guilty to Grand Theft. It was back to the penitentiary for Masters; he and his accomplice would serve the same sentence, up to 5 years in prison.

Some might think that robbing a priest is as bad as it gets, but there is more to the story. At the time Father Robinson was being robbed, he was also being investigated for the murder of a Roman Catholic nun, Sister Margaret Ann Pahl.

Father Robinson and Sister Margaret Ann served the church together at Mercy Hospital in Toledo. It was said there was friction between the two, and on the day before Easter in 1980, the 71-year-old nun was found choked and stabbed to death in the sacristy of the hospital chapel.

Strong but not conclusive evidence pointed to 42-year-old Father Robinson as the killer. Over two decades would pass before cold-case homicide detectives re-opened the investigation. With the use of new forensic technology, and an abundance of circumstantial evidence, the priest was arrested on April 23, 2004.

Father Robinson's trial began on April 21, 2006, and lasted three weeks. The murder of a Roman Catholic nun by a Catholic priest was believed to be the only one of its kind, and drew international media coverage from Court TV, CNN and other media outlets.

On May 11, the jury of seven women and five men only took six hours to find the priest guilty of murder. He was sentenced to 15 years to life in prison.

The Toledo Blade newspapers religion editor, David Yonke, covered the trial. Yonke later authored the nonfiction book, "Sin, Shame, & Secrets," detailing the shocking murder and trial.

Dec. 30, 1975, 2:45 p.m.
Interview with Charles Caldwell Jr.

Before we had a chance to approach Charles Caldwell Jr. he made a call to the Ottawa Hills police and told Chief Wechtel that he wanted to talk to us about the Ottawa Hills murders. Caldwell made the call from the Lucas County Jail, where he was incarcerated and awaiting trial for robbing the Holland Tavern with Masters. Chief Wechtel told Caldwell we would come and talk to him.

As we entered the jail, I said, "This is beginning to become a habit with us, chief." I never like jails, even though I knew we were going to be there yet again talking to prisoners. I had this feeling of confinement, almost claustrophobic. As I have said many times before; there are two things in life I would not want to live without – my health and my freedom.

A deputy showed us to a small interviewing room to await Caldwell.

It wasn't long before the deputy returned with Caldwell. "Just knock on the door when you are finished," he said. I gave him a nod and the deputy closed the door behind him.

"How are you doing, Charles?" I said.

"Could be better."

"We know why you are here in jail Charles, but that is not what we want to talk to you about. We want to talk to you about your friend, Richard Arterberry. You called and said you had information about the Ottawa Hills murders, and that is why we are here."

Caldwell said he met Arterberry at a friend's house on Amherst Drive, in June 1975. He said while he was living with two girls on Broadway Street in Toledo, around mid-September, Arterberry came by and asked if he wanted to break into a house with him. Arterberry said they could get $10,000 by robbing two old ladies who lived there.

"I thought Arterberry was just talking about burglarizing the house and stealing the money; I assumed the ladies wouldn't be home," he said.

Caldwell went on, "Arterberry and I have done other burglaries together, but I can't tell you where, because you might arrest me for them." Even though we would have liked to have cleared the other burglaries, we didn't push the issue for fear of scaring Caldwell out of giving us the information he said he had about the murders.

"Arterberry and I talked about the burglary during the next several days," Caldwell said. A few days passed, and then he saw Arterberry at Walt's Den. He said Arterberry was a bartender there and Arterberry again brought up the burglary. But on this occasion he told him that they might have to kill the two women who lived at the house. Caldwell said Arterberry told him the $10,000 would be from an insurance policy.

"Arterberry never told me where the old ladies lived or how we were going to get paid from the insurance policy," he said. "When I found out the burglary included killing the two old ladies, I told Arterberry I did not want anything to do with it." Caldwell said he was interested in making some money, but was not a violent man and would never hurt anyone. When Arterberry mentioned murdering the old ladies, he knew it was time for him to bail out. "Stealing some money and property is one thing, but murder – no way."

Caldwell said that about three days later, he and some friends went to see Arterberry at Walt's Den. They wanted to buy some marijuana and knew that Arterberry sold it at times. He said

Arterberry took them to a nearby garage where he sold them a pound of marijuana. Arterberry had about three pounds of marijuana Caldwell estimated.

After they returned to the bar he asked Arterberry about the burglary. He said he didn't want to get involved but was curious about it. Arterberry told him the burglary had already been carried out. "I didn't ask him if the old ladies were home and were murdered – I was afraid to," he said.

"The next day I saw in the newspaper that two old ladies had been found murdered in their Ottawa Hills home. Even though Arterberry never told me he murdered the women, I knew he had," Caldwell said.

"Did you know Patricia and David Wernert?" I asked.

"Yes, I met them and knew they were friends of Arterberry, but I did not know they were involved in the murders, or any other crimes, with Arterberry."

Before Caldwell was taken back to his cell, I asked if he would testify against Arterberry in court, and he said he would. Caldwell never asked for anything in return, but most criminals awaiting trial are hopeful their cooperation will result in some consideration when they are sentenced. However, no favors were extended by the prosecution. This was probably because of the seriousness of Caldwell's charges - he had robbed the Holland Tavern with a shotgun, and the potential of serious physical harm to his victims was present.

Dec. 30, 1975
Meeting with Robert Johnson

It was a busy day; as soon as Wechtel and I walked the short distance from the jail to my office the phone rang. It was Robert Johnson, who was in the Lucas County Jail awaiting sentence on two felony charges. Johnson said he had information about one of the people who murdered the women in Ottawa Hills. "I'll be right there," I said.

I smiled at Wechtel: "Chief, guess what? We are off to the jail again. I have another prisoner who wants to talk about the murders."

I knew Johnson from arresting him several times in the past. I always treated the criminals I dealt with honestly and with the demeanor of a friend. The recidivism with criminals is common. I knew the chances of arresting the same criminals from time to time were likely, so I never burned my bridges. If you treat them without respect, they will never share an interview with you in the future. The way you solve crime is from gathering information from people who have knowledge about the crime, and those who know what happened often are criminals. They are the ones who hang with the people who committed the crimes; many times, they can assist in solving the case.

As we left the police station heading toward the county jail, I asked the Chief if he was ready for another interview.

"Why not, it's become our second home. Lately, we have spent more time with criminals than our families."

"What do we have this time?" the chief asked.

"There is an old burglar friend of mine in jail who says he has information about one of our murderers."

With notepads in hand, we entered the jail. By this time the guards treated us like family, and took us straight to the interviewing room.

When Johnson was brought into the room, he greeted me like an old friend.

"How's it going, Robert?" I asked.

"Not bad, Stiles ... it has been a long time."

"I know. I was hoping you were staying out of trouble."

"It's all right. I just got jammed up, but it's not too serious."

"Good. What do you have for me, Robert?"

Johnson said he was housed in the same cellblock as David Wernert and had been talking to him about the murders. "He told me that his attorney cautioned him not to admit anything about the murders to anyone in jail, because they could testify against him later in court." Wernert told him that he doesn't have to worry about his wife testifying against him, because a wife can't testify against her husband.

Johnson said Wernert was worried about the taped statement he gave to me, and added that he didn't remember what he said because he was on the drug Librium when he gave the statement. "Wernert told me that Richard Arterberry mentioned to him and his wife, that he murdered David's mother and his grandmother. Wernert said he and his wife were not involved in the murders."

"He kept telling me the same story, and then told me he would pay me $200,000 if I would testify in court that he told me this," Johnson continued. Wernert wanted him to testify that he told him he and his wife were not involved in the murders. It was apparent that Wernert was preparing a defense pointing the finger at Arterberry as the only guilty culprit.

Johnson said Wernert told him his brother was going to post $20,000 bail for him and his wife, and that if he would testify in court for them; he would give him $200,000 after the trial. Wernert told him his mother and grandmother were wealthy and when he and his wife were found not guilty, he would inherit their money, and then would pay him the money for testifying.

"Is there anything else you can tell us?" I asked. Johnson said no, "That is all he told me, and that is all I know. What I told you, Stiles, is the truth."

As Johnson was led back to his cell, I said, "Take care of yourself, Robert, and let this be the last time I see you like this."

"You don't have to worry, Stiles. This is the last time you'll see me in jail."

Johnson had never been involved in any violent crimes. I had known him and his family for years - he didn't finish school and took to the streets. Even though he promised he would stay out of trouble, I knew it was probably too much to hope for.

Jan. 2, 1976, 2:20 p.m.
Interview with William Francis Sturm

William Sturm, 29, was held in the Lucas County Jail for aggravated burglary when he told his attorney he had information about the murders of Harriett Wernert and Velma Bush.

Attorney William Bingle contacted me and said his client may have some helpful information concerning the murders. Arrangements were made for Sturm to be brought to the police station for questioning.

On Jan. 2, Chief Wechtel and I questioned Sturm in the presence of his attorney.

"I am in the same cellblock with David Wernert, and at night we sleep in the same cell," he said. Sturm said they became friends and spent most of the day and into the night talking. "During the second day we were together, he started telling me about the murders of his mother and grandmother."

Sturm said Wernert told him he had been a lieutenant in the U.S. Army. While stationed in Vietnam, Wernert said his duty was to organize and plan search, seek, kill, and destroy missions. He bragged about how he planned those missions, and said his Army experience helped him in the planning of his mother's and grandmother's deaths.

Wernert said his wife wanted to kill his mother, because she wanted them to move from their house on Christie in Toledo to their house on Emkay Drive.

Sturm said Wernert further told him his mother threatened to damage their credit ratings if they refused to move.

Wernert said he, his wife, and Richard Arterberry discussed killing Harriett, and that Arterberry said he could take care of the job. Sturm said Wernert appeared to be fonder of his grandmother, Velma, because the original plan was just to kill his mother, Harriett.

"David told me that all of them - he, Patricia, and Arterberry discussed and agreed to murder Harriett," Sturm said. On the day the murder was to be carried out, Wernert said he drove Arterberry to Ottawa Hills in his employer's company van. When he and Arterberry arrived, his mother was in the yard. He said they went there on the pretense of getting some tires out of the basement for his race car

Wernert told Sturm that he left Arterberry in the basement until going upstairs later to kill Harriett. He told him that at the time the murder was to take place; he and Patricia were going out to eat with Patricia's employer.

Sturm asked Wernert what they were going to give Arterberry for killing the women, and he said they had not promised him anything, but they had talked about going into business together.

Wernert said they discussed buying a yacht club in Luna Pier, Mich., adding that his mother owned 6 percent interest in the club. David also told Sturm that Arterberry might have stolen $10,000 in bearer bonds from his mother's home.

Sturm said Wernert did tell him that Arterberry admitted stealing a diamond watch and some other jewelry from the Ottawa Hills home, and Arterberry later gave the jewelry to Patricia.

Wernert also confirmed to Sturm other facts in the case.

According to Sturm, Wernert said he was afraid they were going to lose their attorney, Peter Wagner. His brother, James Wernert, was supposed to loan them $20,000 for lawyer fees, but he couldn't come up with the money, and Wernert was worried they would have to rely on a public defender.

He said their son Davey went to live with his brother James in California, but had been returned to Toledo. The boy was staying at the Lucas County Children's Home until foster parents could be found. Wernert said his son would inherit half of his mother and grandmother's estate if he and his wife were convicted of the murders.

"After his attorney started visiting David in jail, David quit talking about the murders," Sturm said. He said it appeared to him that the attorney must have told Wernert not to talk to anyone in jail about the murders.

I asked Sturm if he would be willing to testify to what he told us and he said he would.

The statements Wernert made to Sturm were very damaging for the defendant. I told Bingle that we would bring his client's cooperation to the attention of the prosecutor handling his case.

Afterwards, Chief Wechtel and I discussed the overwhelming evidence we had accumulated against the defendants. We had come to the end of the evidence trail, and now it was in the hands of the prosecutors and the court.

The murders of Velma Bush and Harriett Wernert were two of

the worst I have seen. Chief Wechtel and I talked about how greed can overcome the trust and love of one's mother and grandmother. The blind trust Harriett Wernert and Velma Bush had for their son and grandson had been betrayed, and now they lay dead in their graves.

22
Motion To Suppress Hearing

A motion to suppress hearing by the defense attorney is an attempt to suppress certain evidence offered to the court by the prosecution. The defense attorney, through his motion, is attempting to prevent the evidence in question from being used during the upcoming trial. In order for the judge to rule that the evidence is inadmissible, the defense must show that it was illegally acquired.

On Friday, April 16, 1976, at 9:25 a.m., a motion to suppress hearing was initiated by defense attorney Arthur James on behalf of his client, Richard Arterberry, before Judge John J. Connors Jr. in Lucas County Common Pleas Court.

James stated that the basis for the defendant's motion was that he was denied access to counsel, in violation of Ohio law, and that he believed the evidence would prove that his client was also denied access to a lawyer until after a statement had been made.

James' contentions were that Arterberry had asked for an

attorney prior to his statement taken by me, and that I promised a lesser charge of manslaughter, instead of the more severe charge of aggravated murder, if he would give the statement.

James asked that the statements be therefore ruled inadmissible and that all the evidence obtained through and after the confessions be ruled inadmissible. If the confessions were ruled inadmissible, evidence obtained as a result of the confessions would also be inadmissible.

James' only witness was Arterberry. Arterberry contended that he had James' private unlisted home telephone number in his wallet and that the wallet was in another pair of pants at the Wernert home when we arrested him. He said he asked if he could change his clothes and get his wallet, but I would not allow him to do this. He said while at the police station he again asked for his wallet, and asked that someone get it from the Wernerts' home, so he could call his attorney. He said I refused his request.

Arterberry's second contention was that I promised him the lesser charge of manslaughter if he gave me a confession. The aggravated murder charges he was indicted for, including the three specifications added to those charges, carried the death penalty. The specifications were that the offense was committed for hire; that the offense was committed while committing aggravated burglary; and that the course of conduct involved the purposeful killing of two or more persons.

Arterberry claimed that when I was taking the tape recording of his confession to the murders, I stopped the recording when I asked him if he had been promised anything to make the confession. He said I stopped the tape because he answered that I had promised him a reduced charge if he confessed, and then told him he was not cooperating.

Arterberry said I backed up the tape to the beginning and started over again, but this time claimed he had not been promised anything. During his testimony, Arterberry did not give a reason why he would continue his statement after being made the promise, or why during the second statement of his rights he would now agree he had not been promised anything. He gave no reason why he didn't demand that his lawyer return if he thought he had been promised a reduced charge, but then wasn't.

Arterberry said when the tape was rewound and started again, and his rights were again given by me, he waived all his rights, and when he was asked if he had been threatened, forced, or promised anything, by me or Chief Wechtel, he said no; he was giving the statement of his own free will.

He admitted that I asked him if he had conferred with his lawyer prior to giving me the tape statement, and that his attorney advised him that if he wished to make the tape statement, he had his consent.

Prior to taking the tape recording I asked attorney James to sit in on the confession, but he declined. He said his client was willing to give me the taped confession, but he would rather not sit in.

The evidence James presented to support his client's second contention was the testimony of James R. Thompson, a recording engineer with Hanf Recording Studio in Toledo. James hired Thompson to examine the tape recording to see if the tape had been stopped during the Miranda rights portion of the interview.

Thompson had examined the tape on April 26. To protect the integrity of the tape recording, James, prosecutor Darrell Van Horn, court recorder E.A. Holewinski, and court bailiff Gary Wilson, witnessed the examination.

Thompson testified that he has been a recording engineer for about 16 years.

"My duties consist of recording for making television, radio commercials, films, soundtracks for slide films, cassette duplicating, and masters of phonograph records. The equipment we use consist of Ampex tape recorders, Scully cutting lathe, Recordex cassette duplicating equipment, and Magnasync 16mm transfer. It is my responsibility to operate all this equipment," he said.

Thompson said he was told to look for a stop or a start on the tape. He said he first looked for a skid mark of the capstan starting on the tape, anywhere other than at the beginning. He said when the capstan is spinning and clamps the tape with the idler wheel it leaves a little skid mark on the tape.

"Did you find a skid mark?" James asked.

"No, I did not."

Thompson said the next thing he did was to listen to the cassette tape, and watch the pattern of it on an oscilloscope. He said if the tape is started or stopped, it will make an electromagnetic pop most of the time. If there is an audible pop you will also see a change in frequency on the oscilloscope.

James asked if he found an electromagnetic pop during his examination of the tape. "No, I didn't."

Thompson next changed his equalization, which is like a tone control, so he could listen for more high frequencies. He said tapes normally have a hiss to them, and the room tone is in the higher frequency range.

"Did you find a change?" Mr. James asked. Mr. Thompson said he discovered a hiss change at the point in the tape where I said something about Ottawa Hills. This change on the tape was actually after I had already given Arterberry his rights.

Thompson was asked what could cause the hiss and he said room tone, such as a blower in the room, a furnace turning on or off, a door being opened or closed, a person moving, the tape recorder microphone being moved or the tape being stopped at that point and recorded over.

During cross examination by prosecutor Van Horn Thompson was asked, "You found a drop off in the tape hiss near the words by Ottawa Hills, and you are stating it may have been caused by an opening door, a ventilator turning on or off, a person or persons moving in the room, a movement of the microphone, a change in atmospheric pressure, or it may have been caused by re-recording the tape?"

Thompson said, "That is right."

Van Horn finished by saying, "You have no way of knowing today what or which one of those things actually caused what you heard."

"No, I don't," answered Mr. Thompson.

During my testimony, I said that I had read Arterberry his Miranda rights, verbally, in writing, and on tape, five times after his arrest -

first at the Wernert house while executing the search warrants, later while taking his confessions about stealing the Porsche, then about the murders of Harriett Wernert and Velma Bush.

I testified that he waived his Miranda rights each time, and never asked for an attorney, until after I took a verbal confession from him concerning the murders. It was after his verbal confession concerning the murders that he requested attorney James, and he was granted that request. Arterberry's taped confession about murdering the women was taken after he talked to his attorney and with the consent of his attorney.

Chief Wechtel testified he was present at the Wernert house when I arrested Arterberry for the stolen car, and he witnessed me read him and the Wernerts their Miranda rights. He testified that Arterberry voluntarily admitted the stolen car was his and gave me the key to it. Chief Wechtel said Arterberry never asked for an attorney or to use the telephone.

Wechtel further testified that the day following Arterberry's arrest, James gave us permission to take Arterberry for a ride so Arterberry could show us where he threw the shoes he wore during the murders, and where he threw the murder weapon, from the stolen car. The chief said this was done with the knowledge and consent of the attorney, and that Arterberry waived his rights verbally and in writing while acknowledging that his attorney also gave consent.

Chief Wechtel said he was also present when I questioned Arterberry at the county jail on Dec. 1 and again on Dec. 3 at police headquarters. He said we questioned Arterberry about the murders and clothing he wore during the murders. Wechtel said on all occasions, Arterberry was given his rights both verbally and in writing. He said Arterberry always waived his rights, and never indicated he wanted his attorney present. Wechtel said he never mentioned he had been promised any reduced charges.

Again, Arterberry never asked for an attorney until I asked him to give me a tape confession concerning the murders. On Thanksgiving morning he had already given me a verbal confession involving himself in the murders, but afterwards he decided he wanted to talk to James before giving a tape recorded confession. It was at that time I summoned Attorney James.

James talked to Arterberry and then asked me if I had promised him a reduction in charge if he confessed. I said absolutely not. I told him that only the prosecutor can consider reductions, but James and I did discuss the possible charges Arterberry could be charged with, and he even researched those charges from my Ohio Criminal Law Handbook.

Sometimes a suspect being questioned will ask what he will be charged with, or if there is a possibility he could be charged with a lesser offense if he cooperated. I tell him what charges could be placed but any reductions would be up to the prosecutor. I say I don't have the authority to reduce charges and that if he did cooperate, I would let the prosecutor know.

During the hearing, Van Horn called the jailers who booked Arterberry on the morning of Thursday, Nov. 27. The purpose of Van Horn's questioning was to determine if Arterberry had requested a telephone call after his arrest.

Robert Pribe acknowledged he was present when Arterberry was booked that day. He said he was not the person who booked Arterberry, but was working and present that morning.

"Could you tell the court what procedure is followed when a man is booked at the city jail?" Van Horn asked.

Pribe explained that the time, date, names of the arresting officers, the man's name, and the charges are logged in the arrest record book. His personal property is taken from him and logged in the book, and then he is told he has the right to make a telephone call.

Van Horn showed Pribe a copy of the booking sheet for that day. Pribe identified it as the one used to log Arterberry's information.

"Is there a telephone located in the booking area of the city jail?" Van Horn asked.

"Yes sir, we have four of them in the jail," Pribe said.

"What notations, if any, do you make on the booking document regarding that phone call?"

Pribe answered that if the prisoner makes a phone call, it is stamped in the book, "phone call made." If he doesn't, each turnkey has his own way of recording that a phone call was declined. He said he just writes "no phone call wanted," and he puts his initials next to his comment.

Van Horn asked Pribe if he recalled making such an entry on the booking page for Arterberry. "Yes sir," Pribe responded.

Van Horn handed Pribe the booking sheet and asked Pribe to repeat the notation regarding Arterberry's entry. He said the entry states, "No phone call wanted."

"Did you make that entry?"

"Yes, sir," responded Pribe.

Van Horn asked what the charges listed in the log were. Pribe said a charge of Grand Theft Auto was listed as the original charge when Arterberry was booked, and the charges of murder were added later.

Van Horn said he noticed the charges of murder were in a different handwriting and done with a different pen than the grand theft charge. Pribe said he was not the person who added the murder charges.

Defense attorney James asked if the telephones in the jail were pay phones. Pribe said one was, and three were not.

"So, if a man doesn't have a dime, he can still make a call?" James asked.

"Yes, sir," replied Pribe.

James said the handwriting in the log about the telephone call request appeared to be written by someone other than the person who booked Arterberry. Pribe said another jailer booked Arterberry, but he was the one who offered the telephone call, and who made the notation about the call.

James asked, "Where were you when Arterberry was logged in?"

"I was in another area of the jail when my partner booked Arterberry," Pribe said.

James asked Pribe if he was sure he offered Arterberry a telephone call and if he was sure Arterberry refused.

"I talked to him personally about the telephone call," Pribe said.

Van Horn's next witness was jailer William West.

West was asked the same series of questions. He said he was on duty the morning of Nov. 27 when Arterberry was booked.

Officer West said Arterberry was brought into the jail where he was fingerprinted. His name, social security number, date of birth, sex, race, and occupation were placed on the blotter, along with the charge of grand theft auto.

Van Horn asked West if the entries were made by him, and he said yes.

The prosecutor showed West the booking sheet he had marked for evidence, and West identified it as the log sheet he was talking about. He pointed out the arrest number that identified Arterberry, and he pointed out the Nov. 27 date and time of 4:50 a.m. as the date and time Arterberry was booked.

"After a prisoner is booked, is there any particular procedure followed at the city jail regarding phone calls?" Van Horn asked.

"Yes sir. After the prisoner is booked, all his personal statistics are recorded in the log book, his personal property is removed and a receipt given, then he is asked if he would like to make a telephone call."

Van Horn asked if this procedure is done without exception, and West said, "Without exception."

"Was that request made of Mr. Arterberry on the 27th?"

"Yes, sir," West responded.

"What response did you receive from Mr. Arterberry?"

"He said no, he did not wish to make a telephone call."

West said because the charge was a felony, he asked him a second time.

He said Arterberry replied, "No, everyone I know is either in jail or not at home."

Regarding Arterberry's testimony that his wallet with James' private unlisted phone number was in a pair of pants left at the Wernerts' house, I testified I didn't remember Arterberry ever asking for the wallet and that he never requested an attorney at that time.

As mentioned earlier, I recovered Arterberry's wallet from his prior employer, Walter Staerker, owner of Walt's Den, where

Arterberry was a part-time bartender. I recovered the wallet from Staerker who said Arterberry left it at the bar. Upon inventorying the wallet, in the presence of Staerker and Chief Wechtel, neither James' name nor his phone number were found.

The wallet recovered from Staerker had to be the wallet Arterberry was talking about. When Arterberry was booked in the city jail he had no wallet, and when Chief Wechtel and I executed the second search warrant at the Wernerts' home on Dec. 1, in the presence of the murder victims' estate attorney, Edward Hoffman, we found no wallet belonging to Arterberry. While examining pants that may have been worn by Artererry during the murders, we found no wallet.

In support of my testimony, Van Horn called Sandra Harmon to testify.

Sandra Harmon testified that in November 1975 she was employed at Walt's Den.

She said she knew Arterberry for about a year.

Van Horn handed her the wallet and asked her if she recognized it. She said it belonged to Arterberry, and she last saw it at Walt's Den.

At the bar one night, Arterberry told Harmon he was going to leave the wallet in a drawer. She said he was with some other people, and told her he was going to a party and didn't want to carry it with him. The wallet was in the drawer for three weeks to a month, and after Arterberry was arrested, she told Walt Staerker about it. She said she showed him the drawer and he took the wallet.

She said Walt told her he was going to talk with Detective Stiles, and that he would give him the wallet.

During cross examination, James asked if I had stopped the tape recorder during the portion of the tape recording where I asked Arterberry if he had been promised anything, and if it was true that Arterberry had been promised a reduced charge from murder to manslaughter.

I said I never made Arterberry any promises, and I didn't stop the tape recording during Arterberry's confession. There would have been a stoppage in the tape recording at the beginning because

I always test the recording to make sure the conversation is being recorded. I said there is a leader at the beginning of every tape, a blank spot, and conversation cannot be recorded on the leader. After testing the tape I stop and run it back to the beginning. I then start the tape over, and when I hear "testing" I know it is safe to start the recording. By following this procedure, I can be sure none of the conversation is missed on the tape recording.

The next thing I said after Arterberry was read his rights was:

"Okay, are you willing to waive these rights and give me a statement today and tell me the truth about the things that I ask you?" Arterberry replied yes.

I continued: "I'm going to ask you also, have you been threatened, forced, promised, or compelled by myself or Chief Wechtel, or anyone else, to make a statement, or are you giving it to me of your own free will?" Arterberry said, "Yes, I am."

I knew I made no promises to Arterberry about a reduction in charges, but I did feel we may have discussed possible charges the prosecutor could request from the Grand Jury, and perhaps he was confused about that discussion or distorted the conversation to serve his own purpose. It is not in violation of the law to discuss possible charges the prosecutor may request indictments for; it is only a violation to make a direct promise in return for a confession.

After hearing the testimony and considering the facts, I testified to a hypothetical set of circumstances. If while taping Arterberry's confession, he would have said he thought I had promised him a reduced charge I would have stopped the tape recording and would have told him that I do not have the authority to make such promises. If he had any questions after my explanation, I would have contacted his attorney so he could discuss it with Arterberry.

I testified that under those circumstances I would have discussed his concerns, and if Arterberry said he now understood that no promises can be made to him, and if he agreed to continue his statement at that time, I would have started the statement over and again advised Arterberry of his Miranda rights. If he waived those rights, I would have then taken his statement.

If James felt there was an unlawful promise made to Arterberry in the oral confession, why would he allow his client to give a taped confession concerning a double homicide?

The answer was simple, James would not have allowed this, nor would Arterberry have continued to be cooperative with us if he felt I had violated the law and his Miranda rights.

Copycat

Prior to the motion to suppress hearings, Attorney Peter Wagner had represented both Patricia and David Wernert. He approached Judge Connors and requested that a new attorney be appointed for Patricia. He said he felt it would be a conflict of interest to represent both defendants during the trials. Judge Connors agreed and a new attorney was appointed for Patricia. Upon her request, attorney F. Al Wysocki was appointed.

When Wysocki heard that Arterberry claimed his taped confession had been stopped during his Miranda rights, he jumped at the opportunity of a similar defense. But, as with Arterberry's defense, technology proved to be on the side of the prosecution.

Wysocki brought an expert witness from Menlo Park, Calif., Frausto Poza, senior research engineer for the Stanford Research Institute. He was a highly respected engineer in the field of forensic application of voiceprint identification. His credentials were impressive, receiving Bachelor and Masters Degrees from the Massachusetts Institute of Technology. Poza also attended Purdue University as a graduate student and spent time as an electrical engineering instructor.

Poza's major research and support interest was in the forensic application of voiceprint identification; automatic speaker identification; and speech understanding research.

He diligently examined the taped murder confession I took from defendant Patricia Wernert. On June 25, 1976, he testified to his findings.

Poza was asked by Wysocki to examine the tape recording to

determine if the acoustical manifestations of the information on the cassette were consistent with the hypothesis that once the recording was initiated, it was never interrupted, except to turn it over at the end of side one and to restart it on the other side. He was simply examining the tape recording to see if there were any stop-and-go erasures.

Frausto Poza testified that he found a spot on Side One of the tape where there was nine-tenths-of-a-second erasure. He said this was the only erasure he could find. Obviously, less than a second of erasure could hardly have been intentional.

During my testimony, I testified that the only time the tape confessions were out of my possession was when they were given to Margie Hansen, secretary and clerk typist for the Lucas County prosecutor's office. She transcribed the tapes so copies of the transcripts could be given to the attorneys.

Ms. Hansen testified that the tapes were given to her to transcribe. She was asked about the equipment she used, and she said she used a modified machine to transcribe the tape recordings. The machine allows for her to listen to the tape while transcribing the contents. As a result, Poza took a sample from the modified machine and found that the sample matched the nine-tenths-of-a-second erasure on the original tape. His testimony exonerated me from any possible intentional erasing of the taped confession of Patricia Wernert.

When the hearings were concluded, I felt that my honesty and integrity had been questioned. How careful can an investigator be? I had advised not only Arterberry of his Miranda rights each time I questioned him, but David and Patricia Wernert as well. I used the waiver forms, all signed by them after I read their rights. This same procedure was recorded on each tape-recorded confession.

During the subsequent hearings, the defendants' attorneys used every possible reason to suppress the confessions:

Patricia Wernert was under the influence of drugs or alcohol when she gave her statements; Arterberry was promised leniency if he confessed; his and Patricia's tape recordings were erased and played over.

The attorneys also asked the judge allow for a change of venue.

They claimed the newspaper and television coverage made it impossible for their clients to receive fair trials, and that any potential juror's mind would be tainted by the media exposure. They claimed their clients were denied counsel before the confessions were taken. Arterberry's attorney even asked that he be given a competency hearing.

The court psychiatrist did examine Arterberry, and Judge Connors surveyed the newspaper articles and TV footage before rendering his decision.

He ruled there was insufficient evidence to indicate the taped confessions were obtained unlawfully, and therefore, they were admissible.

The judge also ruled that the examination of Arterberry by the court psychiatrist produced no evidence that Arterberry could not understand what was taking place.

Judge Connors said after examining the newspaper articles and TV footage he found no evidence that the defendants could not receive a fair trial in Lucas County and ruled against a change of venue.

And the judge ruled that Patricia Wernert's contention that she was under the influence of drugs – Valium and Librium – at the time she was given her Miranda rights was not substantiated by the evidence, and therefore, did not warrant a finding in her behalf.

It is well known that when defense attorneys don't have a case, and the evidence is overwhelming, they attack the police investigation.

Even though I continually deal with these tactics, I can never get used to having my honesty and integrity questioned. Although I am not thin-skinned, I knew I would have to contend with the same allegations during the upcoming trials. They didn't have any defense – they had to attack me and Chief Wechtel, especially me, because I was the one who obtained the confessions.

The defense attorneys and their clients had to go to trial - the charge was aggravated murder with specifications for the death penalty. If convicted, the accused would face death by electrocution.

23

The Trials Of The Decade

It was Monday, Sept. 13, 1976, at 9 a.m., and the trial of the people who committed Ottawa Hills' only murders was to commence this late summer day.

Until then, there had never been a case in Lucas County where three defendants, charged with the same offenses, were tried in three separate courtrooms at the same time.

Richard Arterberry, David Wernert, and Patricia Wernert were all charged with the aggravated murders of David's grandmother Velma Bush, and his mother, Harriett Wernert. They were charged with committing a dastardly crime against two elderly women, and now they would answer to the people.

The blind trust of a mother and grandmother led to the betrayal of that trust. Greed resulted in the murders of these innocent women in the confines of their own home.

Judges, prosecutors, and defense attorneys were calling the proceedings the trials of the decade. Murder and mayhem were expected to occur in big cities, but not in the tranquil village of Ottawa

Hills. Many of the more affluent people of the area moved to the village to avoid violent crimes, and now their private world had been invaded. Some of those same people were spectators in the courtroom this day – they wanted to see those responsible punished.

Security in and around the courthouse was more noticeable than usual, as attorneys, family members, friends, and interested citizens made their way to the courtrooms. They were packed to capacity with spectators who came to witness the trials of the decade.

Most of the witnesses would testify at all three trials, and that was the main reason for the trials to run simultaneously. The witnesses could move from courtroom to courtroom eliminating the need for them to return another day.

All three defendants requested a trial by jury, and the selection of jurors was to be made by the prosecutors and defense attorneys in each of the Common Pleas courtrooms.

Richard Wayne Arterberry was to be tried before the Honorable John J. Connors Jr. The assistant prosecuting attorneys were Anthony G. Pizza: and Darrell Van Horn Jr. Pizza earned his law degree from the University of Toledo in 1950, and became an assistant prosecuting attorney in 1951.

Pizza had been an assistant prosecutor for over two decades and was considering running for the office of his boss, Harry Friberg. Friberg had announced he would retire after this term in office and supported Pizza as his replacement. Pizza was a fire-and-brimstone prosecutor who loved his job and was a champion of the people. Although he had a gruff voice and firm appearance, he was a scholar of the law with a pleasing personality.

Van Horn graduated from the University of Toledo in 1972, and was a newer member of the prosecutor's staff. He was intelligent, aggressive, and poised, an upcoming star in the office. His boyish face may have given the appearance of inexperience, but that was deceiving. His abilities were far beyond his years.

The defense attorney representing Arterberry was Arthur F. James. James attended law school at Columbia University, graduating in 1956. He had been practicing law for almost 20 years and was well known in the legal community as a thorough and professional attorney.

The second courtroom would be the setting for the trial of David Ernest Wernert before the Honorable Robert V. Franklin. The assistant prosecuting attorneys were Henry G. Harris and David O. Bauer.

Harris graduated from the University of Toledo in 1970 and was an experienced prosecutor. He had a reputation of honesty and fairness. He organized his witnesses and evidence to line up with the elements of the crime, and then presented his case.

Bauer had recently graduated from the University of Toledo. His interest was working with the prosecutor's office in the criminal division. Friberg recognized his intellectual talents and desire to become a strong member of their staff. Bauer didn't let his boss down; he was up to date with this case and prepared for trial.

The defense attorney representing David Wernert was Peter J. Wagner. Wagner had been around awhile – graduating from the University of Toledo in 1971. He was a go-to criminal attorney for the wayward denizens of our community, and had a reputation of success.

The third courtroom was that of the Honorable George M. Glasser. This would be the scene of defendant Patricia Nicole Wernert's trial.

The assistant prosecutors were James D. Bates and Robert J. Gilmer Jr. Bates was a University of Toledo graduate. He had a personal respect for the village of Ottawa Hills because he worked part-time as a police dispatcher there while attending law school. He later was an intern for the Lucas County prosecutor's juvenile division. He became one of the office's sharpest prosecutors.

Bates was the senior criminal division prosecutor of this team and a strong advocate of the office. He had no desire to defend criminals – he wanted to incarcerate those who were a menace to the community. Unfortunately for the criminals, he was good at his job.

Gilmer was relatively new, a 1975 University of Toledo graduate, a bright young man with lots of energy. A good second chair, he was prepared when jury selection began.

Patricia Wernert's defense attorney, F. Al Wysocki, graduated from the University of Toledo in 1973. He worked almost two years for the Public Defender's office before going into private practice.

I felt comfortable with the prosecutor's team. They were the "Dream Team" of the `70s. Their boss and mentor, Melvin Resnick, worked with them in preparing their cases and throughout the trials.

The judges presiding over the cases were intellectual, experienced, fair-minded adjudicators. Judge Connors graduated from Ohio Northern University in 1956. He was a highly respected judge who was fair to both sides. Arterberry would be tried in his courtroom.

Judge Franklin, a 1950 graduate of the University of Toledo, had a reputation as a no-nonsense judge. He was a strong advocate of separating courtroom jurisprudence from personal friendship. He would preside over the trial of David Wernert.

Patricia Wernert would face Judge Glasser, who obtained his law degree from the University of Toledo in 1953. He was known as a fair and knowledgeable judge. Both prosecutors and defense attorneys thought highly of him.

As the simultaneous trials began, spectators pushed their way into the standing-room-only courtrooms.

More than 150 potential jurors withstood the rigid preliminary examination from the prosecutors and defense attorneys until 12 were chosen for each trial. Once the jurors were seated, the trials began.

Opening statements were next, with prosecutors and defense attorneys outlining what they hoped to prove during the trials.

The prosecutors had strong cases. Each defendant had made confessions, not only incriminating themselves - but implicating their co-defendants as well. All the elements of the crimes were contained in their confessions, further supported by the arsenal of witnesses and evidence the prosecutors had at their disposal.

This was the only time in Lucas County Common Pleas Court history that three co-defendants were tried at the same time in three separate courtrooms. That the defendants were charged with the most severe of charges, aggravated murder with death penalty specifications, made the trials all the more exciting.

Assistant prosecutor Van Horn laid out Arterberry's case for the jurors by telling them what the state intended to prove.

"The evidence, and Richard Arterberry's tape recorded confession, will prove David Wernert took Arterberry to the Emkay Drive home of Harriett Wernert and Velma Bush on the afternoon of Nov. 18, 1975. Arterberry followed the plan he, David Wernert, and Patricia Wernert worked out by hiding in the basement until evening. When he walked up the stairs from the basement to the first floor of the home he was armed with a crowbar given to him earlier by David Wernert. Arterberry confronted Harriett Wernert by the front door and struck her on the head with the crowbar. After downing Harriett he attacked Velma Bush in the kitchen with the same crowbar," Van Horn said.

"Arterberry committed the murders for hire with no more compassion then a butcher in a slaughterhouse," Van Horn continued. He said Arterberry fled the scene in Harriett Wernert's car and abandoned it behind the Kroger store in the parking lot at the Westgate Shopping Center. There he picked up his car he had left earlier. He sped out toward the country on West Central Avenue - throwing the murder weapon and his bloody shoes out the window along the way.

Arterberry's attorney, Arthur James, told the jurors that the only evidence linking his client to the murders was his client's tape-recorded confession, and that it was taken under questionable circumstances. He said I had changed my story about the taping of Arterberry's statement and it would be up to them to decide whose version of the statement is true.

As the opening statements in Patricia Wernert's trial began, assistant prosecutor Bates said the case would show Mrs. Wernert participated in the planning of the murders. He said witnesses testifying during the trial will show she tried to hire different people to commit the murders so she could get control of Harriett Wernert and Velma Bush's estates. The jewelry taken from the Emkay Drive home was hidden by Patricia Wernert and her husband in a crawl space under the dog kennels at the Trilby Animal Hospital where Mrs. Wernert was employed. Bates said testimony and the evidence will show the jewelry belonged to the dead women.

Patricia Wernert's attorney, F. Al Wysocki, said he intended to prove there was no physical evidence to tie his client to the killings. He said he would also produce character witnesses in Mrs. Wernert's behalf. He added he would show that the tape-recorded confession taken from his client by me was coerced, and that further, his client was under the influence of alcohol and tranquilizing drugs at the time of her confession. Wysocki said the statements about killing the women were meant as a joke, and shouldn't be taken seriously.

When opening arguments began in the David Wernert trial, assistant prosecutor Bauer said the witnesses and the evidence would show that the Wernerts hired Arterberry to murder David Wernert's grandmother and mother. He told the jurors they would hear the tape-recorded confession from David Wernert admitting that he and the others planned the murders and that he gave Arterberry the crowbar used to kill the women.

Defense attorney Wagner said his client's tape-recorded confession to me was a lie and that the only reason he gave it was because of threats made against him and his family by Arterberry. He said David Wernert only took part in the murder plot after being threatened by Arterberry.

The excitement began as witness after witness paraded to and from the courtrooms. Many of the witnesses were members of the police community, business people, scientific experts, and members of the coroner's staff.

Some of the prosecution witnesses knew the defendants personally – perhaps making their testimony difficult as the defendants watched from the defense table.

One by one the witnesses testified as to what they knew. Maybe it wasn't easy, but they were steadfast, displaying a sense of duty.

As each of the witnesses testified and the evidence was introduced, Chief Wechtel and I watched as our investigative results unfolded for the court. It was gratifying to see what had once been a confusing set of circumstances come together and be told like the narrative in a Joseph Wambaugh crime novel.

Ottawa Hills Sgt. David Anmahian testified that on the night of Nov. 19 he and Officer John Nyitray were dispatched to 2130 Emkay to check on the safety of the occupants. Upon arrival they found the side door ajar and a back door off a screened-in porch forced. The door glass had been taped and broken.

They entered the house and found Harriett lying by the front door and Velma on the floor in the kitchen. Both women had been bludgeoned to death with a heavy instrument, and several deep gashes were observed on the top of their heads.

"Officer Nyitray and I backed out of the house stepping in the same footprints as we entered," Sgt. Anmahian said. It was obvious by the amount of blood on and around the women, and the stiffness of the bodies, that they were dead. We didn't want to contaminate the crime scene so we went outside the house and made the necessary calls to the police dispatcher. After summoning the paramedics, we notified Chief Wechtel, the coroner, the prosecutor's office, the evidence technicians, and the Toledo detectives for assistance."

Lt. Joseph Eich testified he heard the calls to the dispatcher and sped to the scene. There, he organized the duties for the officers to accomplish and assisted in protecting and processing the crime scene. "We searched the inside of the house and the outside area of the premises for the murder weapon, and any other evidence that may have been left by the killer," he explained. They interviewed neighbors but no one had seen or heard anything. The search for the murder weapon proved fruitless and it appeared the murderer had taken precautions to cover up any evidence.

Ottawa Hills Fire Department paramedics were summoned. Robert Deeds and John Dawley testified that when they arrived the victims were dead. They were the first on the scene, but the ladies had been dead for awhile. The firemen felt bad - their job is to save lives, but in this case there was no hope.

Coroner Harry Mignerey testified he and his investigator, Joseph Inman, examined the bodies at the scene. He later examined the bodies more thoroughly at the morgue and found Harriett Wernert had been bludgeoned with what appeared to be two different weapons, a crowbar-type tool and a hammer. "She had been struck with such force, her skull was fragmented," he said. He pointed out that Velma Bush's injuries appeared to have been cause by a crowbar-type weapon as well. "Her injuries were caused by only one weapon," he concluded.

Toledo police crime scene technician Edwin Marok told the jurors how he and state crime scene technicians William Dailey and James Hockenbery searched the Emkay house for evidence. "The window in the back door was taped and broken and the house had been ransacked," he said. He said they made record of the surroundings by taking photographs. The pictures were introduced to the court for the jurors to examine.

Marok described how they found the house and bodies of Harriett Wernert and Velma Bush. Harriett was laying face down by the front door and Velma was in the kitchen on her back with her legs drawn up to her chest. There was a lot of blood in the area of the bodies and both women had deep gashes to the back of their heads. No murder weapons were found and the only latent fingerprints lifted belonged to the victims and family members. "We could tell the killer wore gloves because we found finger and hand impressions throughout the house, but the impressions left no ridge details indicating the murderer wore latex or rubber gloves."

Sgt. Richard Zielinski, supervisor of the Toledo Police crime laboratory, testified that he examined the hammer I recovered at the victim's home. He said he found a very small amount of blood on the hammer, but there was an insufficient amount to distinguish what blood type it was.

Officer John Nyitray took the witness stand and confirmed what Sgt. Anmahian testified to earlier. He testified how they were dispatched to 2130 Emkay and discovered the bodies. While searching for witnesses he spoke with a neighbor and was told Harriett Wernert owned a '70 red Ford Mustang. Nyitray found the car was missing from the victims garage so he put out a police broadcast searching for the car.

The car was located behind the Kroger store at Westgate Shopping Center in Toledo, by a mall security guard, David Axilrod.

Axilrod testified that he notified both the Toledo and Ottawa Hills police departments. Toledo Officer John Zawisza arrived at the scene and was met shortly thereafter by Ottawa Hills Officer Paul Hanslik. The car was processed for evidence, as was the murder crime scene, by state crime scene technicians William Dailey and James Hockenbery. Testimony indicated that no conclusive evidence linking a suspect to the murders was discovered either at the Emkay home or in the car.

Witness Don Bedra testified that he was friends with Patricia and David Wernert and knew Arterberry. He saw them with the red Porsche they admitted was stolen from where David worked.

Bedra observed strange behavior from Patricia: She played up to him and wanted to have sex, claiming she and David were no longer intimate. She professed to be friends with people in the Mafia, and inquired whether he would be a "hit man" and kill someone for her. She offered to pay him $4,000 to do the job, but would not divulge the target until the job was done.

Bedra was never told who Patricia wanted murdered, but suspected it might be Harriett Wernert, because she mentioned several times to him how much she hated her. She would tell him she wished both Harriett and Velma would die so she could get their inheritance.

Bedra's brother, Craig Bedra, testified that he also knew the Wernert's, and their live-in friend Arterberry. He said while hanging out at the Wernerts' home, Patricia made a comment that she would not mind knocking off the old ladies. David and Patricia said it would be nice to have their money so they could get more involved with their racing car team. Patricia did most of the talking, he said.

Craig, too, said Patricia played up to him and wanted to have sex, but he also declined. Craig was staying with the Wernerts during this period but moved out and quit hanging around with them.

Both Bedra brothers said Arterberry was staying with the Wernerts and both thought it was strange, especially after learning Arterberry did the killings. They said he attended the funeral with the Wernerts, and even took communion with them. Craig said Arterberry used drugs at times, and on occasion he saw him almost legless from getting high.

Don and Craig Bedra both said Patricia Wernert claimed to be a black witch and said she could cast spells on people.

Dr. Robert Burns, the veterinarian, and his wife Donna testified that Patricia Wernert worked at Dr. Burns' Trilby Animal Hospital and that on the night of the murders they all went to dinner together. They said the Wernerts' son, Davey, babysat for their daughter while they went to eat.

The Burns couple said Patricia had a key to the Animal Hospital because she worked there. They said I told them that Patricia and David Wernert had hid jewelry, stolen from Harriett Wernert and Velma Bush's house, under the kennel of his Animal Hospital. Dr. Burns said he allowed me to enter the building and recover the jewelry. He also gave me a key and I found it matched the one recovered from Patricia.

The Burns' said Patricia didn't like Harriett Wernert and talked often about the inheritance they would receive upon Harriett and Velma's deaths.

Attorney Edward Hoffman, the estate attorney for Harriett Wernert and Velma Bush, said Harriett's estate was valued at approximately $245,000, with the beneficiaries being her sons, David and James Wernert. Velma's estate was valued at approximately $400,000. She bequeathed her home at 2009 Christie St. and $10,000 to her grandson David Wernert. She left $10,000 to grandson James Wernert, and an amount equivalent to the appraised value of the Christie Street home. The majority of the remaining estate would be put in a trust. At the time of Harriett's death, her sons would be the beneficiaries.

Witness Ed Neumann testified he owned Neumann Jewelers. He was shown the jewelry stolen from the home of the dead women. It was the same jewelry recovered by Chief Wechtel and me from the Trilby Animal Hospital where Patricia Wernert was employed, and where she and her husband David hid it after the murders. Mr. Neumann identified one of the pieces, a woman's Harvel diamond 17-jewel watch, as being the one he sold to Harriett's husband, James Wernert on Jan. 12, 1971.

Mr. Neumann said he was able to identify the watch by markings he put on the inside of the watch at the time he sold it. He also identified a receipt showing that he sold this watch and some other jewelry to James Wernert on the same date in 1971.

Chief Wechtel took the stand confirming that proper search warrant procedures were followed.

"Detective Stiles read all of them their rights at the Wernert home before executing the search warrants, and before arresting Arterberry for the theft of the Porsche stolen from Will Dennis Volkswagen. They showed no signs of being under the influence of drugs or alcohol, and they never asked for an attorney or to use the telephone. The police crew transported Arterberry to the Toledo police station, and Patricia and David Wernert voluntarily came with Detective Stiles and me to the station. Richard Arterberry was put into a holding cell at the detective bureau and I stayed with the Wernerts and their son Davey while Stiles interrogated each subject individually."

Wechtel testified that after I obtained confessions for the stolen car and the commission of the murders, all three were charged. He said that after I took a verbal confession from Arterberry, and before I took a tape-recorded statement concerning the murders, Arterberry requested an attorney. He asked for Arthur James to represent him, but we could not locate a telephone number for James. His number was unlisted and Arterberry did not know the number.

"A person knowing the telephone number was finally found and James was called. James came to the station and after talking to his client, gave Stiles permission to take the tape-recorded murder confession." The chief said James left and Stiles took the confession from Arterberry concerning the double homicide. "I was not present during the confessions but have since listened to the tape-recorded statements and have read Detective Stiles reports," he said.

During my more than five hours of testimony in Patricia Wernert's trial, I described how she confessed to planning the murders with her husband and Arterberry. "She hated Harriett Wernert but thought better of Velma Bush," I said. Patricia admitted the inheritance had crossed her mind but sided with her husband's statement that it was really a mercy killing. She told me, because of the women's age and health, they thought they were doing them a favor by having Arterberry kill them.

I testified Patricia said Arterberry gave her the jewelry he stole from the Emkay home. She told me that David and she hid it at the animal hospital. I explained to the jurors she never asked for an attorney, nor did she appear to be under the influence of drugs or alcohol. While taping her confession I never stopped and erased any part of the tape to alter her confession. "Throughout the interview, she was cold and calculating," I said.

Witness Sue Johnson was not a person interviewed by Chief Wechtel and I during our investigation. She was discovered by the prosecutor's while talking to other witnesses in preparation for the trials.

Ms. Johnson testified she knew Patricia and David Wernert for five years. Patricia often spoke of how she disliked Harriett and wished she would have a car wreck, burn, and die. Patricia had told her that she only married David for his money and talked about David's inheritance from his mother and grandmother as her inheritance. She said Patricia badmouthed her husband and belittled him in front of others.

Johnson said Patricia bragged she was a witch and could cast spells on those she did not like. She claimed she could do this to get back at them for some reason, and to get what she wanted. "Patricia had an occult room in her house decorated with candles on an altar," according to Johnson. "Patricia said she belonged to a coven in Bloomfield, Mich., and had cast a spell on her former employer, forcing him to commit suicide." Her former employer was veterinarian Dr. Robert Sass - and he did commit suicide.

Johnson said Arterberry attended the funeral of the dead women and she too thought it strange that he sat in the front row with the Wernerts and took communion with them. It was odd that any of them would take communion and pretend to cry at the funeral after proclaiming so much dislike for the women.

Patricia Wernert took the stand in her own defense, first describing why she allowed her taped confession. "I was under the influence of drugs and alcohol when Stiles questioned me," she said. The whole murder plan was a joke; Arterberry was just supposed to scare the women so they would agree to move out of the big house on Emkay and live with her and David.

Patricia said that after the murders, and because of the stress she was under, she obtained a prescription from her pharmacist, 50 capsules of Librium at 10 mg. each. She said on the morning of Nov. 26, and up until Chief Wechtel and I executed the search warrant for their home and took them downtown, she took the Librium, Valium, and drank straight shots of Crown Royal whiskey.

On cross examination by prosecutor Bates, Mrs. Wernert admitted she had made the taped confession, and everything on the tape is what she said, but now claimed she only said those things because Arterberry threatened to harm her and her son Davey if she didn't say she and her husband encouraged him to commit the murders. "Arterberry carried a gun, and after the murders he kept in close contact with me so I couldn't turn him into the police. Besides being in fear of Arterberry, I was under the influence of alcohol and drugs when I made my statement to Stiles."

Bates methodically destroyed her explanation. He pointed out that there were several times when Arterberry was not around her, and that she could have notified the police on any one of those occasions. She countered that if she told the police, Arterberry still could get to her son.

Bates pointed out that when she was taken downtown, she and her son were with the police and Arterberry had been arrested, so there was no reason she could not have told the police of Arterberry's threats at that time. "You didn't tell them because there were no threats," Bates said.

"You attended the funeral of your victims, sat in the front row of the services with your husband and Richard Arterberry, and then took communion with them," Bates said. "At the police station, when finishing your meeting with your husband and Arterberry, and before being placed in your jail cell, you kissed David on the cheek while giving Arterberry a long, hard kiss on the lips. Those aren't the actions of someone scared for their safety."

For the first time during her testimony, Patricia didn't reply.

When asked to explain her involvement in witchcraft, Patricia Wernert said she studied theology at the University of Heidelberg while her husband was stationed in Germany during his Army career. She admitted reading many books on witchcraft, talking to Craig Bedra, Sue Johnson, and others about casting spells on people; having an altar of candles in a room in her house, and having someone play dead in a casket on Halloween. But she fell short of saying she was actually a witch. She admitted she told people she was a witch and had rigged séances with the help of others.

At Halloween parties, she would have someone in the attic make weird noises and move things attached to strings, but that was all in fun. She said she has tried to move things with meditation, and practiced this as a form of relaxation while in jail.

Patricia said she did not belong to a coven. She studied witchcraft and had group discussions about witchcraft with friends. Her husband said she was a black witch – a bad witch – but thought he told her that in jest.

"I don't see a lot of difference between a black witch and a white witch, a witch is a witch," she said. "I think the definition of witchcraft is to believe in the supernatural."

It was obvious Patricia didn't possess the supernatural powers she had tried so hard to achieve. She was not a witch – just an evil person.

Witnesses were called by defense attorney Wysocki in an attempt to further prove Patricia Wernert was under the influence of alcohol and drugs at the time of her confession and arrest.

Dr. Irving Sherman testified for the defense. He said he was a consultant chemist with a Bachelor degree in pharmacy and pharmaceutical chemistry, a Masters degree in chemistry and biosciences, and is a doctor of biochemistry, physical chemistry and life sciences. He said he obtained all of his degrees at Purdue University.

Dr. Sherman testified to the definitions of the tranquilizers Librium and Valium, and to the time it would take for the drugs to dissipate in the body. He said that if Patricia Wernert had taken the quantity of tranquilizers and alcohol that she testified she took, and at the times she said she took them, it was his opinion she would have been under the influence of those drugs and alcohol at the time she gave her confessions.

On cross examination by Bates he agreed he had no personal way of knowing what drugs and alcohol she may have taken, and that he could only testify to the effects they would have had if she had taken the quantity she said she took.

Prosecutor Bates asked Dr. Sherman if Patricia Wernert had taken the amount of drugs and alcohol she claimed she had taken, and in the time frame she described, would that induce her to lie?

Sherman said even if Patricia had taken the drugs and alcohol she claimed to have taken, it wouldn't induce her to fabricate a story or to lie. In response to Bates' next question, Sherman said the drugs wouldn't affect a person's sleep and would actually have a tendency to calm a person down and tend to relax them.

Bates called City jail matron Florence Morgenstern in rebuttal and she testified she was present when Patricia Wernert was booked, and she did not appear to be under the influence of drugs or alcohol. She stated that Patricia was offered the use of a telephone and refused; Mrs. Wernert said any calls that needed to be made would be made by her husband David.

Other prosecution witnesses were called to rebut testimony by Patricia Wernert and her witnesses.

Pharmacist Shale Dolen said it was his opinion that if Patricia had taken the alcohol and drugs she said she took, and had taken them during the times she testified to, they would have been out of her system by the time she was interrogated about the murders.

Perhaps the most damaging witness to Patricia's claims of being under the influence was prosecution witness Dr. Shui-Chin Chen, a toxicologist at Toledo Hospital.

Chen said he had a Bachelor of Science degree in chemistry from the University of Taiwan and a Masters and PhD in toxicology from Massachusetts Institute of Technology. He said he was the associate director of pathology at the Medical College of Ohio, was in charge of toxicology and their laboratory.

Chen explained that toxicology is a multiple discipline to study a toxic substance - how they act in the body, and how the body gets rid of them, or how they do injury as well as how to determine the substances.

Chen was given the same set of circumstances as Sherman and Dolen as to Patricia Wernert's testimony about the amount of drugs and alcohol she had taken before being interrogated. Chen testified that if Wernert had taken the amount of alcohol and tranquilizers she said she took, and if she had taken that quantity in the timeframe she said she took it, she would have died before my interrogation.

Defense attorney Wysocki called Fausto Poza the senior research engineer from Stanford Research Institute. He was asked to testify about his examination of the murder tape recorded confession taken by me from Patricia Wernert. Wysocki contended that during the taping of Patricia's murder confession I had altered the tape.

Poza had testified at the earlier motion to suppress hearing. He repeated that testimony. He said while examining the tape he found less than one second eraser on the tape. His examinations discovered the eraser was caused by the prosecutor's office secretary when she was transcribing the tape. He agreed with the prosecutor that the less than one second eraser would not have altered the statements on the tape.

"It was a mercy killing," explained David Wernert while giving his tape-recorded confession to me.

"My mother and grandmother were always complaining about being sick and having trouble getting around their house. They were having problems caring for themselves, and they were becoming more of a burden to me. They refused to move and were determined to stay in their big house. I tried to get them to move to a smaller place where they could care for themselves better, but they refused to leave their home in Ottawa Hills."

David confessed that he, Patricia, and Arterberry planned the murders, and it was Arterberry who bludgeoned the women with a crowbar he gave him.

"I hid Arterberry in their basement around noon on Nov. 18 and he was to go upstairs and kill them while my wife and I were having dinner with my wife's employer, veterinarian Dr. Robert Burns, and his wife. We arranged the time of death and the dinner for the same time to establish an alibi for me and my wife. I never promised Arterberry anything for committing the murders but I had discussed going into a bar business with him.

After the killings Arterberry said the murders went according to plan. He gave Patricia the jewelry he stole from the house and she placed it in an Avon jar. We took the Avon jar to the Trilby Animal

Hospital where Patricia was employed and I buried it under the dog kennels."

David drew a map for me showing where he hid the Avon jar and Chief Edward Wechtel and I later recovered it from exactly where he showed me on the map.

The testimony of witness William Sturm caught the attention of David Wernert's jurors when he told them David had confessed the murders to him while they were lodged together in the Lucas County Jail. Wernert told Sturm he planned the murders as he had planned military search-and-destroy missions against enemy sympathizers, while serving as a U.S. Army lieutenant in Vietnam.

Sturm said David told him that he, his wife, and Arterberry planned the murders of his mother and grandmother but it was Arterberry who killed the women. He told the same story he had given to Chief Wechtel and me during our prior interview with him.

David Wernert took the witness stand in his own defense, with direct examination conducted by defense attorney Peter Wagner.

On the stand Wernert contradicted his earlier taped confession in which he admitted that he, his wife, and Arterberry planned and carried out the murders of his mother and grandmother.

"My statement that the murders were intended as mercy killings was false," David said. He only made the statement because he feared for his life and that of his son, he said, explaining that Arterberry threatened their lives if he did not claim to be involved in the murders. David recanted what he told me during the tape recording, denying he had any part in the murders. "I only said the things Arterberry told me to say because I feared Arterberry might kill me and my family," he said.

Wernert said he tried to persuade his mother and grandmother to move to an apartment that would be safer and easier to maintain, but they refused to leave the house and neighborhood they loved.

"Patricia and Richard Arterberry devised a scheme to scare them into moving, and reluctantly I agreed with the plot after being assured the women would not be harmed. Arterberry was to hide in their basement, and after they fell asleep he was to make pry marks on the door to simulate an attempted burglary.

"On the day of the murders, I took Arterberry to the house and hid him in the basement. My wife and I went out to dinner with some friends, and when we returned home, Arterberry was there and told us the plan had been carried out. I did not know my mother and grandmother had been murdered until the following evening when the police contacted me. My wife and I had called the women several times during the day and received busy signals. I called the police and ask them to check on their safety – this is when the murders were discovered."

"Arterberry told my wife and I that he murdered the ladies and threatened to kill us and our son if we told on him. Arterberry carries a gun and we feared for our safety. Later I learned from Arterberry that my wife was actually involved in the murder plot and they fed me tranquilizers to keep me quiet. My wife gave me so many tranquilizers during the day, and the night Stiles and Wechtel served the search warrant and interrogated us, I felt like a zombie."

Wernert's taped confession was so believable while coming from his own mouth that it was inconceivable that a jury of four men and eight women would even consider that he made the statement under duress. That taped confession, coupled with the recovery of the stolen jewelry his wife got from Arterberry, and which David and Patricia hid at the Trilby Animal Hospital where she worked, made a tight case.

Prosecutor Harris cross-examined Wernert. He denied he confessed to the murders of his grandmother and his mother to his former cellmate William Sturm, but did admit that while serving in the Army in Vietnam, he had participated in assassinations of enemy sympathizers.

Harris picked apart Wernert's contention that he only made the taped confession under duress from Arterberry. Harris pointed out that if that were true, he had many occasions to go to the police and have Arterberry arrested. "Arterberry was not with you and your family at all times," Harris pointed out.

Shuffling from courtroom to courtroom, it was time for me to testify at Arterberry's trial.

I testified that during the taping of Arterberry's confession, he described how he had met Patricia and David Wernert through their mutual interest in car racing. He described how he got caught up in their plan to kill David's mother and grandmother.

"The Wernerts kept telling me how sickly the ladies were to the extent that I began to think killing the women would amount to doing them a favor," Arterberry said. On the day he was to commit the murders, he said he and David followed the plan plotted earlier by all three of them.

"David took me to the Emkay home and hid me in the basement. I was armed with an 18-inch crowbar given to me earlier by David. I had taken several tranquilizers before we left the Wernerts' home to build my courage, and while waiting for the prearranged time to murder the women I fell asleep on the basement floor. At 7 p.m. I went upstairs because I knew the Wernerts were establishing their alibi while eating dinner with Patricia's boss and his wife at Kings Cove restaurant in Temperance, Mich.

"David's mother was watching television and his grandmother was in her bedroom off the dining room. I sat down on the hallway stairway leading to the upstairs and played with Harriett's dog. I was having second thoughts about the killings and started to walk toward the front door when Harriett Wernert came out of the living room to the hallway. I struck her twice on the head with the crowbar.

"I was going to leave when Velma Bush came from her bedroom and walked through the kitchen carrying a flashlight. I struck her several times on the head. I taped the back-door window and broke the glass to make it look like a burglary. Then, I dumped drawers out to give the impression the house had been ransacked. I stole some jewelry, took the keys to Harriett's red Ford Mustang, and fled in the car. I left the stolen car behind the Kroger store at Westgate Shopping Center and retrieved my car from where David and I had left it earlier.

"I drove out Central Avenue at speeds of over 100 mph, and while speeding along the countryside, I threw the murder weapon and my shoes out the window. I stopped and hid the jewelry in some weeds and drove back to the Wernerts' home where I was staying. I later took Patricia to where I hid the stolen jewelry and gave it to her."

I testified that when I asked Arterberry what he expected to get for committing the murders he said nothing definite had been promised him, but he and the Wernerts had talked about going into some sort of a business venture together. He said he felt he would be taken care of when David inherited his grandmother and his mother's estate.

I spent the entire day testifying at Arterberry's trial. I said that before and during my interrogation of Arterberry, he was afforded every opportunity to call and speak to his attorney, and I even granted his request to speak to the Wernerts.

I responded to prosecutor Van Horn's question on whether I had made any promises to Arterberry, or offered him leniency to get him to make the taped confession. "Absolutely not, Arterberry made a free and voluntary confession," I said.

During cross-examination by defense attorney James, I was accused of promising Arterberry a reduced charge if he confessed. He contended that when Arterberry mentioned the promise during the tape-recorded confession, I stopped the tape, and after erasing the promise, turned the recorder back on.

I testified that I never made any promises to his client and that the only time I recalled stopping the tape was when I tested it to make sure the recorder was functioning properly.

I thought to myself that it should be pretty obvious to the jurors that everything was handled properly, or James would not have allowed his client to give the tape-recorded confession. Again, I hoped the jurors remembered that Arterberry had already given me a verbal confession admitting the murders, and this was before he requested an attorney. I further felt the jurors would take note of the fact that Arterberry did give the taped confession played in court, and on the tape he waived his rights and stated that he had not been threatened, promised anything or compelled by me or anyone else to make him give the statement. He also acknowledged on the tape that he had spoken with his attorney before giving the statement, and was told by James that he could make the statement.

In addition, I had asked James to set in on the taped confession but he declined.

The tape spoke for itself - Artereberry was not promised anything to make him give the statement.

The attempt by James to discredit me and the tape-recorded confession continued when he again requested the testimony of James Thompson, the recording engineer. Thompson had testified earlier at the motion to suppress hearings that he was asked to examine the tape for a stoppage.

He again testified that a hiss noise on the tape could have been caused by several things - a re-recording, a movement in the room, movement of the recorder microphone, or an air handler coming on and off.

During the motion to suppress hearing, Judge Connors ruled that there was insufficient evidence to indicate that an erasure had occurred on the tape recording, or that I had promised Arterberry leniency if he confessed. Therefore, the taped confession was admissible to be played at Arterberry's trial.

Arterberry's friend Charles Caldwell Jr. revealed Arterberry's intentions when he told his story to the jurors.

Caldwell said he met Arterberry through some people in June 1975 and they became friends. One day he and Arterberry were talking and Arterberry asked him if he wanted to break into a house with him. He claimed they could get an easy $10,000 by robbing two old ladies living in the house.

He said he thought Arterberry was talking about burglarizing the house while the women were not home but during further discussions was told they might have to kill the old ladies.

Caldwell said when he found out murder might be involved he told Arterberry he didn't want any part of it. Arterberry never told him who the targets were but later told him the burglary had been carried out. He said the next day after their conversation he saw in the newspaper that two old ladies had been found murdered in their Ottawa Hills home, and even though Arterberry never admitted to the murders he felt he was guilty.

When asked if he knew the Wernerts, Caldwell said he met them through Arterberry, but had no idea they were involved in the murders.

City of Toledo jailers Robert Pribe and William West testified that they were working on Thanksgiving morning, Thursday, Nov. 27, when Arterberry was arrested and placed in custody. They both said that Arterberry did not appear to be under the influence of drugs or alcohol and that he was offered a telephone call but refused. The jailers also testified that when Arterberry was booked in the city jail, he had no wallet.

When Arterberry took the stand in his own defense, his statement was much different than that given to me during his taped confession.

This time, Arterberry denied murdering Harriett Wernert and Velma Bush, and said he was lying when he made the taped confession. He said he agreed to go along with a plan created by the Wernerts to scare the women into moving from their home.

"The plan was for David to take me to the Emkay home and hide me in the basement," Arterberry said. Contrary to his earlier confession, he said the plan was for him to just scare the ladies. He now said he was not supposed to murder the women but rather handcuff them and ransack their house to frighten them.

Arterberry continued: "After David left me in the basement I fell asleep, because I had taken some tranquilizers earlier. I slept for several hours before going upstairs where I found both women were already dead. The rear-door window had been broken and the house had been ransacked. I picked up a hammer from the basement and searched the house for an intruder. No one except the dead women and me were in the house, so I returned the hammer to the workbench in the basement, and then fled the house in Harriett Wernert's Mustang in order to avoid being accused of the murders." He also denied stealing the missing jewelry.

Arterberry said he never denied the murders to the Wernerts because he didn't think they would believe him. He said after his arrest he confessed to me about beating the two old ladies with the crowbar because I told him the Wernerts had implicated him in the killings. He said he told me what I "wanted to hear" after I promised to attempt to arrange a reduction in his charge from murder to manslaughter. He said when he mentioned the promise on the tape recording; I erased that portion of the tape and started the statement over again.

Under cross-examination by prosecutor Pizza, Arterberry stated he lied about murdering the women because he felt that was his only hope. He said the manslaughter charge sounded a lot better than being charged with murder.

Pizza went over all the things that I had just testified about and asked Arterberry how he could explain his taped confession being supported by the facts and evidence produced at his trial. Pizza pointed out that Arterberry and the Wernerts admitted that they planned the break-in and that he carried it out. He admitted to hiding in the ladies' basement, handling one of the murder weapons - the hammer with blood on it - and to stealing Harriett's car.

"You have admitted everything during this testimony that you admitted earlier, with the exceptions of stealing the jewelry, breaking the door glass, and murdering Harriett Wernert and Velma Bush," Pizza said. "The ladies were all right when you hid in their basement, but were dead when you came upstairs to handcuff them, is this what you want us to believe?"

Pizza pointed his finger at Arterberry and shouted, "By your own admission, you murdered those two innocent and helpless women, and now you are trying to save yourself. Your confession to Detective Stiles is the true statement, and you are trying to cover that up by accusing this fine detective of wrongdoing!"

Arterberry stared straight ahead while prosecutor Pizza returned to his seat. Pizza, known to his friends as "Tony," was a true crusader for truth and justice. He appreciated and respected the attorneys and police he worked and served with, and allowed his feelings to be known when their integrity was questioned.

With the completion of Arterberry's testimony, all three cases were now before the jury. The evidence and photographs submitted to the court were entered into evidence by the judges in the three courtrooms, and now it was time for closing arguments.

"The taped confession from Richard Arterberry tells it all," prosecutor Van Horn said. "Which statement of Arterberry should you believe - the one he gave to Detective Frank Stiles soon after his arrest, or the one he gave in court? I point out to you, members of the jury, that his statement to Stiles matches the evidence in the case, and the one he gave in court is self-serving - made up only after he realized the possible consequences."

Arterberry's attorney, Art James, said this was a curious case in which both the prosecution and defense claimed that Arterberry had at times told the truth, while at other times he lied.

James pointed the finger at me, who had taken the confession and who made the arrest of his client. James questioned my credibility by saying Arterberry only confessed after a promise of leniency.

"The son and grandson of the victims solicited the help of Richard Arterberry to carry out his and his wife's plan to murder the women," Bauer, the assistant prosecutor, said. Bauer told the jury that David Wernert never claimed to have been coerced into making his statement and that he made it voluntarily and of his own free will.

"It was only after Richard Arterberry threatened his life and the life of his son, that his client David Wernert, told Detective Stiles, he took part in the plot to murder his mother and grandmother," defense attorney Wagner said. Wagner said Wernert's testimony was the true account of what happened and said David had no advance knowledge of the murder plans.

Assistant prosecutor Gilmer pointed out to the jury that Patricia Wernert helped in the planning of the murders, and arranged for an alibi to protect both her and her husband from detection on the night of the murders. "Just remember what Mrs. Wernert said on the taped confession given to Stiles and you will see how she collaborated with her husband and Arterberry to murder Harriett Wernert and Velma Bush," Gilmer said.

"Detective Frank Stiles asked leading questions when the taped confession was taken from Patricia Wernert, who was under the influence of alcohol and tranquilizing drugs at the time of the questioning," defense attorney Wysocki contended. He said his client had no motive to participate in the murders because she was not a direct beneficiary in Harriet Wernert and Velma Bush's wills.

It was Monday, Sept. 20, and the trials had lasted seven grueling days.

Now that closing arguments were finished, the judges in each courtroom provided the instructions of law to the jurors. When the instructions were completed, each judge retired the jurors to start their deliberations. The jurors for each defendant were sequestered immediately after the judge's instructions and would remain so until they returned their verdicts. The jurors would be confined to their individual jury rooms and hotel rooms if a verdict was not reached at the end of the day.

It was decided among the judges that no verdict would be announced until all the verdicts had been returned, and then they would be announced in the same time period.

The jurors were released to start their deliberations and tight security would guard over them throughout. Although security is not allowed in the jury rooms or in the jurors hotel rooms, they would stand guard nearby.

Meanwhile, lawyers and spectators congregated to see what each other thought. "Do you think they will be found guilty?" one spectator asked another. "How long do you think it will take?" You could hear the comments flying around the courtrooms and in the hallways. TV and newspaper reporters raced to meet their deadlines, and Chief Wechtel and I went home for some much-needed rest.

The trials were long and exhausting. We had done our job – now it was up to the jurors.

Lucas County Courthouse
700 Adams Street, Toledo, Ohio
Scene of murder trials
Photograph taken by Toledo Police Department photographer
Sgt. Keefe Snyder

Richard Wayne Arterberry Trial

Judge
John J. Connors

Prosecutor
Anthony G. Pizza

Prosecutor
Darrell Van Horn

Defense Attorney
Arthur F. James

David Ernest Wernert Trial

Judge
Robert V. Franklin

Prosecutor
Henry G. Harris

Prosecutor
David O. Bauer

Defense Attorney
Peter J. Wagner

Patricia Nicole Wernert Trial

Judge
George M. Glasser

Prosecutor
James D. Bates

Prosecutor
Robert J. Gilmer

Defense Attorney
F. Al Wysocki

Justice Alice Robie Resnick – Ohio Supreme Court
Hon. Melvin L. Resnick – Sixth District Court of Appeals
At the time of their marriage in 1970, and at the time of the murder trials in 1976, they
were both Lucas County Prosecutor's
Photograph taken in front of the Ohio Supreme Court

24
The Verdicts Are In

The first of the three defendants' verdicts was in. David Wernert's jurors took less than three hours to reach their verdict. They retired to the jury room a little after 3 p.m. and were back at 6 p.m.

"Wow," some spectators exclaimed. Judge Franklin inspected the verdict before sealing the document, as promised. Even though the verdict had been received, attorneys and spectators would have to wait for the verdicts of Patricia Wernert and Richard Arterberry before David's verdict would be known.

Immediately, the speculations began. "Do you think the early verdict means conviction or acquittal?" The attorneys had the same question, but most felt it was a good sign for the prosecution.

People hung around the courtrooms figuring there would be more quick verdicts, but as the hours ticked away, it was obvious the other jurors were taking a close-hard-look at the evidence and testimony. Most jurors sitting on a serious case take their time in examining the evidence and testimony.

Perhaps the reason David Wernert's verdict was returned so

quickly was that there were fewer issues to consider. He never contended there was anything wrong with the taping of his statement, and his confession was so cold and conclusive, it would have been difficult not to believe.

Also, witness William Sturm, the jail-mate of Wernert, gave strong testimony that David had confessed the planning of his mother's and grandmother's murders while they were confined in the Lucas County Jail.

It was getting late, so all the judges in all three cases sent the jurors to hotels for sleeping accommodations. Even David Wernert's jurors were sent to a hotel and would remain sequestered until all the verdicts were in.

Soon after the sun rose on Tuesday, Sept. 21, the jurors were awakened for breakfast and the return trip to their respective jury rooms. By 9 a.m., the jurors in the Arterberry and Patricia Wernert cases were hard at work deliberating.

"Listen, everyone, I have some news," the bailiff in Judge Glasser's courtroom said to the defense and prosecution attorneys still lingering around the courtroom and corridors. "Patricia Wernert's jurors have a verdict."

It was 1 p.m. - Patricia Wernert's jurors had been deliberating for 10 hours and had made their decision.

After all the prosecutors and defense attorneys gathered in the courtroom, surrounded by the packed seats and standing-room only crowd, Judge Glasser inspected the verdict. Once he had examined the document he sealed it and returned the jurors to the jury room to await Arterberry's verdict.

"Well, it shouldn't be long now," prosecutors Van Horn and Pizza agreed. They had tried the case of Arterberry, the actual murderer of Harriett Wernert and Velma Bush. No one was surprised that the jurors in his trial would be out the longest. Even though the evidence against Arterberry was overwhelming, the jurors had a lot of evidence and witness testimony to consider.

Analyzing the physical evidence, examining and rehashing witness testimony, going over and listening to a most incriminating and damaging tape-recorded confession from Arterberry, and considering the many statements from expert witness testimony - takes time.

Pizza and Van Horn weren't wrong. Two hours later, at 3 p.m., after 12 hours of deliberation, the eight men and four women jurors returned their verdict. Judge Connors inspected the verdict then resealed it.

The verdicts were to be announced one at a time – starting with that of David Wernert. The courtroom of Judge Franklin looked like opening day at Cedar Point amusement park. Every seat was filled with spectators while others crammed the aisles and extended out into the hallway.

Chief Wechtel and I sat at the prosecutors' table with Harris and Bauer. Like everyone else, we listened intently for the verdict to be read.

David Wernert was found guilty of two counts of aggravated murder and specifications on each count that the murders were done in the commission of a burglary, that the plan called for the killing of more than one person, and that the murders were done for hire.

Then, the masses moved from his courtroom to the courtroom of Judge Glasser, where Patricia Wernert's verdict would be announced.

She was found guilty of two counts of aggravated murder and specifications on each count that the murders were done in the commission of a felony, that the murders were done for hire, and that the plan called for the killing of more than one person.

As everyone headed for the last courtroom, where Arterberry's verdict would be read, I said to Wechtel, "Two down and one to go."

Arterberry was found guilty of two counts of aggravated murder and specifications on each count that the murders were done for hire, that they were committed during the commission of a burglary, and that the plan was to kill more than one person.

The aggravated murder charges and accompanying specifications meant all three of the defendants faced the death penalty – death by electrocution. The defendants could actually be sentenced to two death penalties each, one for the murder of Harriett Wernert and one for the murder of Velma Bush.

Ohio law also called for a separate hearing to be held for each defendant in order to determine if there existed any mitigating circumstances described by law that would prevent the defendants from being sentenced to death.

The death penalty was mandatory in Ohio following aggravated murder convictions, unless there were certain circumstances showing the victim provoked or induced the murder, the murder was committed while under duress or coercion, or the defendant suffered from mental deficiency or some form of mental illness.

The mitigating circumstances hearings were scheduled for Nov. 22, 1976, for each defendant. Arterberry and the Wernerts would learn their fate: Life in prison or death by electrocution.

Capital punishment has been part of Ohio's history since the conception of the state in 1803. Earlier murderers were hanged by the neck until they were dead. The initial hangings were public, and the killer was hanged in the county in which he committed the act. Eighty-two years later the legislature decided all executions would be held at the Ohio Penitentiary in Columbus.

At the end of the 19th century, executions were changed from death by hanging to death by electrocution. The electric chair was developed as a more humane method of execution. Before then, 28 hangings were carried out at the penitentiary.

"Old Sparky" soon became the nickname for Ohio's electric chair, and during its existence 312 men and 3 women were seated for their last time. The first to die by electrocution was a young man from Hamilton County named William Hass, and the last to die in 1963 was Donald Reinbolt from Franklin County.

Now that the trials were over and the verdicts had been rendered, the judges, prosecutors, and defense attorneys thanked the jurors in each case for their diligent service. The judges told the jurors they had performed ably and well. The jurors were also told they were now free to discuss the cases if they wished, but that they were not obligated to discuss them. As the jurors exited, many acknowledged the trials had been long and difficult, but few would comment further.

When interviewed by a Toledo Blade newspaper reporter, Chief Wechtel said he was pleased the trials had concluded, but there was no satisfaction in convicting people for a senseless crime that should never have happened.

I was interviewed by the same Toledo Blade reporter after everyone had left the courtroom, and when I saw the paper the following morning, the headline and story read:

"The Toledo police officer who felt that his integrity as a police officer had been impugned during the Ottawa Hills murder trials, said he felt he had been exonerated shortly after the verdicts were announced Tuesday."

Detective Sgt. Frank Stiles, whose credibility and integrity as a witness came into question during all three trials, said the evidence in the cases was overwhelming. "It boiled down to the defendants' confessions. Most of the evidence came through the confessions.

Assigned to the Ottawa Hills police department to assist with the double murder investigation, Detective Stiles and Chief Edward Wechtel arrested the trio last November, and then Stiles conducted the taped interviews used as evidence at the trials.

Defense attorneys questioned the validity of the tapes, contending that they had been altered or that the defendants – David Wernert, his wife Patricia Wernert, and Richard Arterberry – were unable to understand their rights because they were under the influence of drugs and alcohol.

The defense attorneys told jurors that the taped statements had been obtained from their clients under what they termed questionable circumstances – that Detective Stiles had coerced the defendants.

Speaking in the dimly lit deserted fourth-floor hallway outside the prosecutor's office in the Lucas County courthouse, Detective Stiles answered the allegations by saying it hurts to be called a liar in court. You know the truth that it is a ploy on the defense attorney's part, but it's still no fun to have your family, friends, and fellow officers read the false allegations in the paper and see it on TV.

"It is a common strategy for attorneys in defense of their clients to do, when they have no other defense, but it doesn't make it any easier.

A case in point is his 8 year old son Carey who told him that he had seen him on television. "They called you a liar," the father quoted his son as saying, "but I know you don't lie, Dad," the boy reassured him.

Those kinds of moments make you wonder if the good we do as police officers outweighs the strain it can put on those you love.

25

Murderers Given Death Penalty

The same hubbub that was present among courthouse denizens during the trials of Richard Arterberry and David and Patricia Wernert continued during the mitigating circumstances hearings.

Monday Nov. 22, 1976 had arrived and the killers would learn whether they would live or die. It had been one year, almost to the day, that they took the lives of David's mother Harriett Wernert and his grandmother Velma Bush.

All the same players were there, the defendants looking as hard-faced as they did throughout the hearings, the prosecutors determined and ready to proceed, and the defense attorneys with less hope than they had in the beginning.

The crowds of legal minds and spectators hadn't diminished – the courtrooms were still jammed to capacity and beyond.

The judges in each courtroom listened to the testimony produced by both sides, as to why mitigating circumstances were sufficiently present or not present, to execute or not execute each defense attorney's client.

A psychiatrist was put on the witness stand by attorney Wagner in an attempt to show that his client, David Wernert, was under duress from the killer, Arterberry, and that may have induced him to go along with a plan by his wife and Arterberry to break into the home of his mother and grandmother in order to scare them into moving.

Assistant prosecutor Harris countered by pointing out that the psychiatrist failed to prove Wernert was coerced into taking part in the crime.

Attorney James tried to convince Judge Connors that the mitigating hearing process required his client to admit his guilt in an attempt to save his own life. James contended that the mitigating circumstances in the law are "illusionary," stating that it is very unlikely that a defendant would be convicted of murder if such circumstances existed, and therefore, his client or any other defendant, convicted of murder, would stand very little chance of avoiding the death penalty.

Wysocki, attorney for Patricia Wernert, presented no testimony or evidence at the hearing, claiming he was in no position to argue mitigating circumstances for something his client maintained she did not do.

Assistant prosecutors Pizza, Van Horn, Bates, Gilmer, Harris, and Bauer pointed out that no evidence or testimony had been produced by the defendants' attorneys that would support sufficient mitigating circumstances which would justify a sentence less than the death penalty.

"Without mitigating factors the court was under statutory obligation to impose the death penalty," Bates said.

At the end of the day, the attempts by friends and relatives, and the expert testimony of psychologist, psychiatrist, probation officers, and other professionals, failed to convince any of the three judges.

Prior to sentencing, each of the defendants was given the opportunity to make a statement. Arterberry read his from handwritten notes.

He contended that the trial against him was an "insult to justice" and that he had not received a fair trial. "My trial and the other two trials were a three-ring circus."

He said the standards of credibility applied to my testimony and his were different, indicating the jurors placed more credibility on my testimony than they did his. "They chose to believe Sergeant Stiles when he said I admitted I murdered Harriett Wernert and Velma Bush, rather than believe my statement in court, that the women were already dead when I found them."

Arterberry expressed his disgust that jurors generally give more credence to a police officer than they do a person accused of a crime.

Insisting she was innocent, Patricia Wernert said she had not received a fair trial. She further contended that she believed her attorney, Wysocki, was hindered when told by the judge that he couldn't send questionnaires' to the jurors who presided over her trial.

David Wernert chose not to make a statement to the court, but through his attorney, indicated he would appeal the conviction.

Now that the mitigating circumstances hearings were concluded and the defendants were given the opportunity to make a final statement, the judges were ready to render the penalties.

They were of the same opinion that each of the defendants tried in their separate courtrooms would be sentenced to death by electrocution.

Judge Franklin set David Wernert's execution date as April 4, 1977.

Judge Connors directed that Arterberry would be put to death on the same date.

Judge Glasser designated April 6, 1977, as the date Patricia Wernert would die.

Court appeals

The appeals process calls for defendants to have the opportunity to present their arguments to higher courts in an attempt to get their cases overturned altogether or to have their sentences reduced.

A defendant can appeal to the Sixth District Court of Appeals and if that is not successful, they can continue on to the Ohio Supreme Court. If still not successful, they can move on to the U.S. Supreme Court.

Many people seem to believe the appeals process is a waste of taxpayer's money, but it is an important part of our legal system. Consider the new technology of DNA: Since the inception of DNA analysis, many incarcerated prisoners have been set free because DNA discovered at the crime scenes proved to be someone else's.

No sooner had the sentencing of the defendants taken place than the defense attorneys started the appeals process for their clients.

Judge Glasser granted Patricia Wernert's request that her court-appointed attorney, Wysocki, be appointed to continue her quest for freedom during the appeals stage.

Judge Franklin confirmed that attorney Wagner would be appointed to handle the appeal for David Wernert.

Attorney James told Judge Connors he believed the attorney who handled Arterberry's appeal should be someone other than himself.

"I believe that another attorney should be appointed so a fresh look of the case and facts can be experienced," he said. James added that he would be available to assist the new attorney preparing the appeal.

Defense attorney Ralph DeNune III was appointed by Judge Connors to handle Arterberry's appeal.

Lucas County assistant prosecutor Julia Reinberger became part of the prosecutors' team, and would assist Van Horn with Arterberry's appeal process.

Richard Arterberry, David Wernert, and Patricia Wernert were sentenced to death by electrocution. Their executions were to be carried out in April 1977 at the Southern Ohio Correctional Facility in Lucasville, Ohio.
"Old Sparky" as the electric chair was known,
would carryout the sentences.
Photograph furnished by the Ohio Historical Society.

26
The Day After

It was the day after the sentencings – I had taken a vacation day. I just wanted to sleep in until 7 or 8 in the morning, instead of getting up at my usual time of 4 o'clock.

I needed a few hours to reflect on the past year – especially the last week. I was having second thoughts about who I was and the profession I chose. During the almost 12 years on the police force, I had seen so much.

My thoughts took me on a roller coaster ride through the past criminal cases I worked on, reminding me of what horrible things people are capable of. While making arrests, I have been assaulted, bitten, spit on, and shot at.

During one arrest, a robber pulled a gun and tried to shoot me point-blank in the stomach, but his gun misfired. During the confrontation I shot the robber in the arm. He fled with me in pursuit and, with the assistance of other officers, the robber was arrested. After he served his time and got out of prison, he murdered an old man in his home during a burglary.

But I also reflected on all the wonderful people I had been fortunate to meet along the way. Anyone in the criminal justice line of work experiences the same thing I was going through, I told myself.

Is it worth it? Does the good I do outweigh the terrible things I see? Is the burden I carry and the stress it has on my family and personal life justify what small contribution I may make? When you feel you have done a good and honest job – made a difference - only to be ridiculed and beat up by defense attorneys for days and months at a time, is it really worth it?

All I wanted to do in my life was to have a family, be employed at something I enjoyed doing, and to make enough money to educate my children and support my family.

I realized that this was the American dream; this is what most people strive for. I knew at an early age that I was not cut out to work in a factory, be a full-time teacher, work a job where I would be confined inside all day, or be in politics.

My father, Eugene Stiles Sr., taught me a lot of things, but two stand out: "No matter how big or small – do it right or not at all," he said. And this: "When you leave a job, leave in good standing – remember you were the one who asked for the job." I am the youngest of nine children and I lost my mother Janie at a young age. But I felt I was lucky to be raised in a big family - the experiences and learning advantages from a big family cannot be duplicated.

I enjoy many things about my job, meeting new people, being pretty much my own boss, learning other people's professions, and most of all trying to help those in need.

Police work, especially the work of an investigator, is like no other profession. Every case is a new experience – no two investigations are the same. I enjoy the continuing education my profession provides, not only keeping abreast of new laws and procedures, but in learning the professions of so many others. Before an investigator can investigate, he must have an understanding of the victim, and many times the victim's business, and how the business operates. He must have a good knowledge of medical terms, the court system, and anything else that may help in reading the minds of the criminal.

As I have said many times, you have to know your enemies in order to understand their antisocial behavior.

Although it is very disturbing at times, I do enjoy digging deep into the criminal mind, to see what makes him tick and try to understand why he thinks as he does and does unthinkable things.

After weighing all the pros and cons of my profession, I got up at 4 o'clock the following morning and went to work.

27

First Day On Ohio's Death Row For Women

In an article from People magazine, dated April 25, 1977, Patricia Wernert described her first day on Ohio's Death Row for women. The headline read:

Pat Wernert's cell is 'the end of the world'

"I'm the new kid on the block," says Patricia Wernert, 34, a schoolmarmish ex-Army wife who is the most recent arrival on Ohio's Death Row for women. "When they brought me here last November I was manacled and handcuffed, then stripped, given a shower and put in a room. I realized then, 'Here I am. This is the end of the world!'"

Mrs. Wernert was convicted of complicity in the brutal 1975 beating deaths of her husband David's 67-year-old mother and 97-year-old grandmother. Prosecutors said the victims, who lived together in the plush Toledo suburb of Ottawa Hills, were killed for a $2 million inheritance. David Wernert and another man are also awaiting execution for the crime.

The tiny cell where Mrs. Wernert passes each day seems light years removed from the Erie, Mich. farm where she grew up. Married a week after graduating from high school, she traveled with her Army officer husband to bases at home and abroad (and attended such schools as the University of Heidelberg). Though she and David Wernert maintain a Death Row correspondence, her deepest attachment is to her 13-year-old son, Davey, who now lives with friends. "He's very impressionable," says his mother. "I don't want him to grow up hating the police."

Mrs. Wernert spends her days reading law books, poring over auto racing magazines (she and her husband owned and raced Triumphs) and writing legal appeals "for some of the girls here." Though she takes tranquilizers and a daily sleeping pill, she can flippantly refer to the electric chair as "ole thunderbolt." She eats her meals with two other condemned women at Marysville. "We joke about it," Patricia says. "Some people think it is ghoulish, but this is the only way to cope. Otherwise we'd be eaten up inside."

Epilogue

Richard Arterberry, David Wernert, and Patricia Wernert appealed their convictions all the way to the Ohio Supreme Court, without success.

The convictions withstood the test of the appeal courts, and the aggravated murder charges and death penalty sentences were final - or so everyone thought.

The U.S. Supreme Court ruled in 1978 that Ohio's death penalty law did not meet the court's criteria and was unconstitutional. As a result of that ruling, 120 condemned prisoners in the Southern Ohio Correctional Facility at Lucasville had their death sentences commuted to life in prison. Arterberry's and the Wernerts' lives were spared by this new ruling.

On Oct. 19, 1981, the death penalty in Ohio was reinstated. After Ohio lawmakers drafted the new law to reflect the strict criteria of the Supreme Court, capital punishment once again became an option in aggravated murder cases. The new law did not affect the Wernerts and Arterberry because their death penalty sentences had already been commuted to life in prison.

Patricia Wernert was even granted a new hearing to again resolve the allegation that her Miranda rights had been violated because she claimed to be under the influence of drugs and alcohol at the time she gave her confessions. A new attorney for Patricia, Mark Shenfield, filed a writ of habeas corpus in federal court more than seven years after her murder conviction.

The hearing was held before Magistrate James G. Carr in the U.S. District Court on March 22 and 26, 1984.

Ohio Assistant Attorney General Richard Drake represented the state. He was assisted by Lucas County Prosecutor James D. Bates. After the hearing, Magistrate Carr ruled in favor of the state and Patricia Wernert was returned to prison.

All three remain in prison. I was told by family members and friends that Arterberry works fixing appliances, David Wernert makes furniture, and Patricia Wernert works in the laundry room. Even though they did not meet the fate they had bestowed upon their victims, they will never be released.

The legacy David and Patricia Wernert bequeathed their 12-year-old son left young Davey's life in turmoil. The boy now had no parents, grandmother, or great-grandmother.

He went to live with his aunt and uncle, Deborah and James Scott Wernert, in San Bernardino, Calif., but that didn't work out, and after two short months he was returned to Toledo. He remained in the custody of the County Children's Home until being placed in a foster home.

In June 1976, young Davey went to live with foster parents Kathy and Robert Jarosz in nearby Walbridge, Ohio. The foster parents had been friends of Davey's parents. Kathy had met Patricia Wernert while both worked for veterinarian Dr. Robert Sass. The Jaroszes were Davey's godparents before the murders, so Davey now had someone who cared.

Kathy Jarosz was appointed guardian of young Davey, subsidized by the court for Davey's expenses. The expenses were to be paid from the inheritance Davey would receive upon his 18th birthday from the estate of his grandmother and great grandmother.

Davey had good direction from his foster parents while in the Rossford school district. Although he was well-behaved and did his share of chores around the house, he had a distance about him, his foster parents told me. He didn't do well in school and didn't particularly like school.

Kathy and Robert Jarosz made a few trips to visit David and Patricia Wernert in prison, and Davey went with them two or three times. The Wernerts never admitted their guilt during those visits and didn't discuss the murders with the foster parents or Davey. A few letters went back and forth, but after Davey turned 18 the communications stopped.

Davey received his portion of the inheritances and moved out of his foster parents' home into an apartment. He quit school his senior year, and spent much of his inheritance on cars.

The Jaroszes said the last time they heard from Davey was just after he moved to Mississippi. They don't know why he moved there, but he did have a girlfriend and perhaps that influenced his decision. The foster parents have not heard from Davey since he moved to Mississippi.

The other heir to Harriett and Velma's estates was Harriett's adopted son and Velma's grandson, James Scott Wernert. He continued to live with his wife Deborah in San Bernardino until he died at age 49.

The lead prosecutor in Arterberry's trial, Anthony G. Pizza, was elected Lucas County Prosecuting Attorney, serving a record-breaking 45 years in the office. He built a reputation as a crime fighter, taking his legal staff from 10 to 50 prosecutors during his tenure. Felony cases rose from 600 to 3,000, and many of the prosecutors he mentored went on to become judges. Mr. Pizza died in 2007 at age 85, and is deeply missed.

Assistant Prosecuting Attorney Darrell Van Horn Jr. served several years with the prosecutor's office before entering private practice. He is now retired.

Arterberry's attorney, Arthur James, is retired, enjoying one of his favorite things, playing the piano at special functions and for friends.

Henry Harris, lead Lucas County assistant prosecutor in the David Wernert trial, retired from the office after 10 years, joined the seminary in 1982, was ordained in March 1986, and now is a minister at St. Timothy's Episcopal Church in Massillon, Ohio.

The second chair at the trial of David Wernert, Lucas County assistant prosecutor David O. Bauer, served many years with the office and is now an assistant U.S. Attorney.

David Wernert's attorney, Peter Wagner, is still in private law practice.

James D. Bates, lead Lucas County assistant prosecuting attorney in the Patricia Wernert trial, was elected a Lucas County Common Pleas Court judge. He married another distinguished Lucas County assistant prosecutor, Julia Reinberger Bates, who became Lucas County prosecuting attorney. She remains in that position today.

The other Lucas County prosecuting attorney in the Patricia Wernert trial, Robert J. Gilmer Jr., now is with the private law firm of Eastman and Smith.

Patricia Wernert's defense attorney, F. Al Wysocki, legally changed his name in March 1979 to Bendel Alan Freeman. He moved to Columbus, and no longer practices law in Ohio. Some who knew him say that his new name stands for "Be A Free Man."

Chief Assistant Lucas County Prosecuting Attorney Melvin Resnick, who assisted the prosecutor's team, became a Common Pleas Court judge and in 1990 was appointed to the Sixth District Court of Appeals. He died on Sept. 11, 2008 at age 81. His wife Alice Robie Resnick, was a Lucas County prosecutor, a Toledo Municipal Court judge, a Sixth District Court of Appeals judge, and an Ohio Supreme Court Justice. She is now retired and lives in Ottawa Hills.

Ottawa Hills Police Chief Edward Lloyd Wechtel is enjoying his retirement with his wife, Pat.

Lt. Joseph Eich became chief of police after Chief Wechtel retired. He too retired, and he and Chief Wechtel still get together with several other retired officers.

The Ottawa Hills police officers who worked on the murder case, Sgt. David Anmahian, Sgt. David Janowiecki, John Nyitray, William Snell, Christian Lopinski, and Paul Hanslik all retired after serving their community with distinction.

CPSIA information can be obtained at www.ICGtesting.com
Printed in the USA
LVOW11*0349140316

479040LV00005B/23/P

9 781432 753924